INTERVIEW
with DESIRE
and
GET HIRED!

HOW TO ACE THE INTERVIEW, SELL YOURSELF & GET YOUR DREAM JOB

Denise Wilkerson, BSN, MHRD, SPHR
Randy Wilkerson, MBA, CPC

Cover Design – Jaycee DeLorenzo
Cover Photos – iStock Photos
Illustrations – Carlos Lemos
Publishing Coordinator – Sharon Kizziah-Holmes

Dandyworx
Productions

Published by Dandyworx Productions, LLC

This book is available at quantity discounts for bulk purchases.
For information, call 1-877-370-2462

ISBN -13: 978-1-7332611-6-6

DEDICATION

This book is dedicated to all of the passionate candidates we have worked with over the past two decades who have shown *desire* throughout the interview process to get the job of their dreams.

INTERVIEW with DESIRE and GET HIRED! is also dedicated to our fathers, David Cottiers and Curtis Wilkerson – two hardworking men who followed their passions. They both overcame challenging circumstances in their youth to achieve successful careers and loving families. We are thankful to them for their encouragement, guidance, and support throughout our lives and in every endeavor.

ACKNOWLEDGMENTS

We are thankful to God for the opportunity to work together as recruiters, authors, and spouses. We are blessed in our relationship with Him.

Thank you to each one of the following individuals for their help in creating this book:

Sharon Kizziah-Holmes – Publishing Coordinator
Holly Atkinson – Editing & Review
Carlos Lemos – Illustrations
Jaycee DeLorenzo – Cover and Book Design
Sherry Haney – Website & Technical Support

Thanks to our friends, family, candidates, and business associates who have helped along the way with your stories.

We hope you enjoy *INTERVIEW with DESIRE and GET HIRED!*

CONTENTS

PREFACE

Thanks for picking up our book! We've spent a lot of time with individuals just like you – people who are highly capable but may need some direction and ideas on how to make their career dreams come true. You may be looking for a resource to learn how to successfully interview and correctly answer the most frequently asked interview questions. That's important. We'll definitely be helping you with those topics in this book. But there's much more to finding your sought-after job.

Not only do you need to understand how to interview and answer questions correctly, you must first determine *if* and *why* you *want* the job. It sounds crazy, but sometimes candidates get caught up in the excitement of an upcoming interview without giving the necessary reflection about the opportunity itself. It sounds counterintuitive but determining *if* and *why* you want the job needs to be conscientiously explored. Yes, it's critically important that you and the employer are a match! We discussed this at great length in our previous book, *HIRE with FIRE: A Relationship-Driven Interview and Hiring Method.* The bottom line is that you don't want just another job— you want the job of your dreams… right?

Consider your career future. Are you interested in a new job because you want to make more money? Are you driven to have more time with your family? Are you interviewing to further your career? No matter how you respond, these areas have one thing in common – it is something you *want*, right?

Some might ask, "Does anyone really *want* to work?" Yet, work brings value, worth, security, and a sense of well-being. No, maybe not every day! Work is hard. Most of us were not born wealthy, so work is a necessity in order to live our best life and support our family. But when there's a career and job fit, it's nice.

I am sure you will agree that at any given point in time, each of us can be in different stages of our careers. Maybe you just graduated, or you are new to a management role and want to continue to climb the corporate ladder of success.

Where is your career today? Are you starting over? Are you content with where you are? Do you want to be promoted to a higher position? No matter where you are at this time, your career will change. Employment and people are not static; they are both in constant flux, changing due to family situations, new innovations, technology, and improvements. Change happens routinely, and as a result, we are sometimes forced to adapt. With layoffs and downsizings, change is often not by choice. For that reason, you need a plan, and that's what we hope to help you accomplish in these next few chapters.

If you noticed, we have frequently italicized the word *want* for extra emphasis. It might sound silly, but actually *wanting* to make your next career move is one of the most important traits that you can show to employers. The right experience, education, and skills are just a few of the traits that employers seek when hiring. However, a person can have the right background and the best education and *still* not get the job. How is that possible? Because no matter how you analyze it, it comes down to this: human beings hire other human beings. And as human beings, we want to know that the person we are extending a job offer to really *wants* the position.

In our book, *HIRE with FIRE: The Relationship-Driven Interview and Hiring Method,* we discuss how human interactions and relationships develop during the interview and hiring process. Throughout the book, we compare the interview process to a personal relationship, such as dating. We relate the two activities (dating and interviewing) because both activities involve feelings. Here is an excerpt from *HIRE with FIRE*:

> *Throughout the interview process, the employer and potential employee will meet to get to know each other better. During this time, they may experience a variety of different feelings similar to the emotions involved in a personal relationship, the nervous energy of meeting someone for the first time, the awkwardness of getting to know each other, or the worry about their first impression. Interviewing, just like dating, involves feelings. By definition, feelings are an emotional state or reaction. Sometimes those feelings bring insecurity. Oftentimes, if we are lucky, they bring us reassurance, enthusiasm and passion. Either way, as human beings, our feelings are an important part of who we are. Although we hate to admit it, our feelings can change our destiny and can cause us to move forward or turn back. Our emotions often guide us into knowing whether or not an anticipated change, such as a career move or a candidate hire, is going to benefit us or cause us peril. This instinctual feeling is known as our gut reaction.*

Managers often make hiring decisions based on instinct and experience, sometimes with limited thought behind it. This gut reaction is critically important. We've all heard how important the first few minutes of an interview can be. This is where an initial favorable (or unfavorable) impression is made. A candidate also has a gut reaction during their first interview. If it's clearly not a match, why continue? If interested, a candidate needs to do everything possible to make sure that their interviewers walk away with a favorable impression of their knowledge, abilities, and interest in the job opportunity. We'll talk in later chapters about how you can make the interviewer's gut reaction favorable for you and how to make it to the next step in your candidacy.

So, how do you alter someone's gut reaction? For over two decades, we have recruited candidates for job opportunities with our client companies. In the course of our work, we have noticed that successful candidates had several traits in common – functionality, integrity, results, and enthusiasm (or as the acronym we refer to as FIRE in our book *HIRE with FIRE*.) Throughout the course of this book, we will reference these characteristics and teach you how to showcase these traits, along with your successes, to potential employers.

As you read, remember this: a person with desire *wants* for something, someone, or some outcome. They are wishing, hoping, longing for this change. Before you go to your next job interview, read *INTERVIEW with DESIRE and GET HIRED!* and take time to find out if you truly *want* the job. If you do, let us teach you how to show the employer you *want* the job – so you get the *job of your dreams.*

INTRODUCTION

Why "DESIRE?"

DESIRE… in other words, a wish and hope for the future. Maybe desire is an odd word to use in the title of a book about interviewing. It makes more sense if you picked up a romance novel, right? Perhaps not. To succeed, you need a strategy, a strong desire, and passion.

You can probably think of several examples in your personal life where you had to work hard, create a plan, and move forward with passion and desire. For some, it may be weight loss, playing an instrument, or excelling in sports. We all have desires, and most of the time, reaching our goal means putting in hard work. But if you truly desire it, your hopes and dreams can come true!

Take, for example, cross-country runners. Now, I have never been skilled at sports, but running seems like it probably wouldn't require a complex plan. Many might think it is simply ready, set, go. However, talk to any runner, and you will quickly learn that it requires desire and a well thought-out plan. When you are competing in an endurance run, it takes just that – endurance.

I remember watching my daughter in junior high compete for her cross-country team. It wasn't easy. There were many days that were a challenge for her. But her interest in running and being a part of a team, coupled with her passion to finish what she had started, outweighed any adversity. That is desire!

Desire is a great word and concept. Some of its synonyms describe it best. Desire involves an appetite, an ambition, a craving, and devotion. True desire helps us reach our goals. If we long to be a part of something or change something in our lives, we will work harder toward that goal. Interviewing for a job takes desire! That is why we used it in our title.

You might think, "I am not sure I even want this job!" And to be honest, you probably won't know until you are two or three interviews into the hiring process. But what if you don't put your best foot forward until the third interview? By then, it may be too late, and you may have missed the opportunity to impress the interviewer.

Our belief is that you should always be ready for that next chapter in your life. Create a plan, polish your resume, understand your skills, be prepared to interview and approach each job with curiosity and DESIRE! But you already know this. That is why you picked up this book. By learning how to interview effectively, you will be ready whenever that dream job presents itself.

We are living in uncertain times. Because of the constant element of change present within the job market, you need to be prepared for the next opportunity. That could be tomorrow! I'm not being negative – just realistic. In fact, a downsize today may result in a better opportunity or career tomorrow. It happens more often than you may think.

To help you get ready for that time, we will be discussing six important steps to take before, during, and after the interview process. As experienced recruiters, we have found that these six particular activities create success and can make the difference in whether a candidate ultimately gets the job or gets the dreaded rejection email.

We will use the word, "desire," as an acronym to help you remember each of these areas as you interview for your dream job. Each letter will represent a key step in the interview process that will help you not only show desire, but also help you sell your abilities to any employer.

With over two decades of recruiting experience, Randy and I will share some of our personal and professional stories to help you understand the importance of these six steps:

D: *Develop Your Brand*
E: *Educate Yourself About the Opportunity*
S: *Show-up & Shine*
I: *Interview with Integrity*
R: *Results*
E: *Enthusiasm*

If you plan and organize each interview around this concept, you will fully engage the interviewer by showcasing all of your preparation and respective attributes. Interviews – and the preparation they require – can be stressful. Having an organized plan and confidence going into an interview can help you remain poised and positive. Following the DESIRE methodology creates a checklist that virtually guarantees that you have covered the key areas of preparation.

♦ CHAPTER ONE

Step 1 – The D in DESIRE: Develop Your Personal Brand

Let's talk more about *you*!

When seeking a job, *you* are the product. Keep in mind that during an interview, you are selling yourself and your abilities to an employer. Just as major companies market the unique features and benefits of their product lines, you must do the same when applying for a job. When you are talking about yourself, remember to talk specifically to your interviewer about what *you* can do for *them*! Their primary interest in hiring you is to improve their organization. If you desire the position, you need to make sure their next stellar employee is *you*. Let's talk about how to make that happen.

To market yourself, you need to create a personal brand. Are you a caring professional registered nurse? A results-oriented sales professional? Maybe a creative software engineer? What skills, personal attributes, education, and past experience make up who *you* are as a career professional?

Creating your own personal brand starts with a professional image and continues throughout your career. This is not a static proposition. It will change with time and be additive in nature as you develop your experience, education, and skill sets. Examples of personal branding include cover letters and resumes, which are tools to help you highlight your unique achievements. Consider these tools as self-advertisements. Let's discuss.

Cover Letters

When applying to a job online, include a formal, well-written cover letter to demonstrate your writing abilities, personality, manners, and intelligence.

A cover letter is one of the tools you can use to sell yourself to an employer. Target your cover letter to fit the job. Don't miss the opportunity. The cover letter allows you to show interest and aptitude to the employer in regard to a particular job opening in which you are interested. Do this by discussing any related background and experience you have that could have direct relevance to their opportunity.

If you are applying online to a job advertisement and there is not a place to upload a cover letter, you may not need it. However, if you want to stand out from other candidates, apply online as usual, but also find a physical address and mail your cover letter and resume to the prospective employer the old-fashioned way. Most companies will try to deter you from applying in-person or mailing applications, but if you put in the extra effort, it may get you noticed over other candidates.

Your cover letter can help you secure an interview. It is important to mention your achievements. Everyone wants to hire a *winner*. A well-written cover letter should pique the interviewers' interest in you by revealing your related past experiences and how those align with their opportunity. Being as specific as possible is also helpful. If you understand the position well, demonstrate this within your cover letter. You can do this by citing examples in your past employment history that will help show how you fit into the role.

Your cover letter, as well as any other document that you present to a potential employer, is a representation of you, as it is a part of your personal brand. If any of your documents are incomplete, lack substance, or contain errors in spelling or grammar, an employer will be less likely to contact you. Ask a professional to review your resume, cover letter, and other documents. Double-check the spelling of names. Let's use my name as an example. I spell it Denise, while others spell it Denice. However, no one spells it Diane. While I am not offended by any of these discrepancies, an interviewer might be and they may not interview you based on this lack of attention to detail. The reason behind their concern is that your potential errors might impact future business and create issues with customers. They are hiring their next candidate to represent their business or organization. It's possible, if not probable, that they may have reviewed over a hundred resumes. No doubt, they're looking for someone that is polished, professional, and can lead their organization to further success. By your attention to detail, you can make it easy for them to select you.

When drafting your cover letter, begin by highlighting your career and explaining how your background, past experience, and accomplishments can benefit their company. To do this effectively, you must have a concrete knowledge of the company. This includes the company history, their mission, and their basic structure and customer base. In a nutshell, know as much about the company as possible. You would be surprised how many seemingly good candidates are eliminated simply because they failed to do any homework. With most company information now online, there is no excuse for a lack of research.

Your cover letter should also have bulleted points, providing key statements that exhibit your skills and attributes and how these could benefit their company. This will draw the interviewer's attention to these important areas. Remember, even in the cover letter, you only have a few seconds to make a positive impression.

Close the cover letter by asking to meet with the interviewer and portraying confidence in your ability to do the job. Ask the employer for the opportunity to meet with them in person. A statement such as, "When we meet, I look forward to discussing the position with you further," is an assumptive close. An assumptive close makes the assumption that the interviewer wants to meet with you. It is a tactic used by the best sales professionals. By making an assumptive close in your cover letter, you show confidence in your product (you!).

The following is an example of how you can structure your cover letter.

Example: Cover Letter (Sales Professional)

First Name Last Name
Address, City, State, Zip Code
Phone Number
Email address

Date

Hiring Manager First and Last Name
Title
Hiring Manager Address
City, State, Zip Code

Re: Job Title

Dear Hiring Manager: (include a personal title such as Ms., Mrs., Mr., or Dr., if possible)

My professional experience and educational background make me a strong candidate for your open position in this territory. Please allow me to discuss a few of the reasons why my background and skills are a match for your organization.
I possess these attributes:

- Proven track record of success
- Five years of successful outside sales experience in business-to-business sales
- President's Club Winner, 2019
- Rookie of the Year, 2017
- Bachelor of Science degree in _____, graduated with honors; G.P.A. _____
- Hunger and eagerness to make money
- Willingness to work hard and strong desire to learn

Outlined in my enclosed resume, I have additional experience selling _____ products to _____. This past experience should prove to be valuable by helping me gain access to more customers. Coupled with my strong work ethic and knowledge of the sales process, these skills will help me exceed the sales goals you set before me.

I look forward to discussing the position further with you. I am confident that when we meet, you will agree that my qualifications and enthusiasm make me a perfect match for this position.

Sincerely,

Your Signature

Your First Name and Last Name

Resume Styles

Cover letters are important, but nothing trumps the importance of a well-crafted resume.

There are several types of resumes – targeted, chronological, functional, and a combination of these. In addition to these types of resumes, a curriculum vitae (CV) is another format that allows for more detailed documentation. A curriculum vitae is typically useful when applying to scientific, technical, academic, or higher education positions.

The most commonly used resume format is the chronological resume. It is easy to read and allows the interviewer to follow your career movements in chronological order. We feel this type of resume is preferred by most employers because it is straightforward. It's by far the most popular format representing approximately 90% of the resumes we view every day.

There are many resume templates available. Some are fancier than others. Pick a style that works well for updating and readability. If your resume is difficult for you to update, it is probably not the best style. Your goal should be a clean, concise, and easy-to-read document with consistent margins and font throughout. Try to become a "neat freak" about fonts, margins, and spacing. Otherwise, there is really no reason to spend so much time developing great content, only to present it in a haphazard format.

As you apply to different companies, your resume will be entered into each company's database or what is now called an Applicant Tracking System (ATS). If your resume is written in a complicated format, it may cause issues when it is imported. Avoid distracting lines and unique or non-traditional spacing. While your resume might look good as a hard copy, a resume needs to be set up digitally to align with today's software and database searching systems. We'll talk more about that when we address keywords later in this chapter.

It's important for prospective employers to readily be able to access and download your resume. Currently, the most widely used formats are Microsoft Word (.doc or .docx) or Adobe (.pdf). We prefer using an Adobe .pdf format prior to submission because it helps with importing.

The following is an example of an easily imported resume. Later in this chapter, we will discuss the components of a resume.

Example: Resume

First Name Last Name
Address, City, State, Zip Code
Phone Number
Email address
Add LinkedIn Address

Summary of Qualifications

Results-driven professional with expertise in relationship building and territory management. Particular strengths include excellent oral and written communication, communicating product knowledge, providing impeccable follow-up, and a commitment to delivering superior service. Analytical, meticulous, detail-oriented, problem-solver with excellent time management and organizational skills. Strong record of managing projects and improving work processes.

Work Experience

Company Name   Start Date – present
Job Title
Short Description of Job

- List Accomplishment #1
- List Accomplishment #2
- List Accomplishment #3

Company Name   Start Date – End date
Job Title
Short Description of Job

- List Accomplishment #1
- List Accomplishment #2

Education

Month, Year of Graduation
Type of Degree/School, Location

Skills/Training/Certifications

Fluent in a language?- add it here.
Received any special training? Add it here along with the year you received the training

Willing to Travel – Open to Relocation

Create a "Winning" Resume

For your resume to stand out against the competition, it has to catch the eye of the reader and grab their attention. The reader should be able to quickly see (1) who you worked for, (2) what you did, and most importantly, (3) how well you did it. Your goal should be for them to see your winning attributes and accomplishments within seconds of skimming the page.

Consider your resume the winning shot in your favorite sport. In other words, your resume and other tools (i.e., cover letter, presentation style, brag book, sales plan) make up the ball you toss, kick, or catch that helps you score enough points to win the game.

Your resume should be a portrait of your skills and abilities. It is essentially your brochure, although it is not intended to be your autobiography or a job description. The purpose of your resume is to market *you* and *your* abilities. Just like your cover letter, your resume should also reflect your "personal brand." Think about what makes you marketable in your field. The "ball" you select to use in this game should be able to endure many critical passes.

We consider your resume the most important tool you will use to sell yourself and your accomplishments to an employer. Think about what you can offer as an employee. Do you have any unique skill sets? For example, are you able to speak another language? If so, you may want to include that in your resume. What makes you different from other candidates that may be applying for the same job?

As you create your resume, make it more than a job description. Create a document that highlights your past accomplishments, education, and skills. Similar to how a company sells a product, your resume should include all the great things about you! Don't just include your duties and responsibilities, but include how well you performed those duties and responsibilities. For example, if you were in charge of frying hamburgers at a local fast food establishment, then you might discuss how many hamburgers you produced per hour, how you cut costs, and if you received an "Employee of the Month" award.

If you haven't realized it yet, we think resumes are critically important! A resume is your first impression to a prospective employer and a poor resume might prevent you from getting an interview. Today's preferred resumes are well-written, purposeful, focused, and brief – highlighting what makes a person employable.

We will discuss how to make your resume stand out, but remember it is never "done." Throughout your career, you will continue to add to and refine your resume. It is a formal presentation of your accomplishments, but it's also a working document that ultimately will collect items of significance for future use. You will find it very useful to note and save important milestones in your career to later present within your resume, so make sure you keep documentation of these career events. Examples might be promotions, awards, special recognition, customer letters, and more. In the sales industry, candidates are expected to present their accomplishments during the interview process. It is usually in the form of what is called a "brag book." In Chapter Five, we will teach you how to create this type of document for your next interview.

Let's discuss some basic information on designing a resume and the components that you will need to include in the document:

Type of Paper
When printing your resume for an in-person interview, we recommend using

resume paper (typically 24 lbs.), which can be purchased at any office supply store. Light-colored paper is easier to print on; typically, light gray, light blue, off-white or white works best. Avoid unprofessional colors (pink, green, etc.). While a pink, scented resume worked well for Elle Woods in the movie, *Legally Blonde*, it most likely won't work for you.

Margins

Margins should be at least 0.5 inch from all sides. Always produce a sample print of your document. This will allow you another view of the formatting and readability of your resume. If you cannot print it easily due to close margin errors, neither can an employer. If you don't have a printer, then make sure your margins are at least 0.75" on the top, bottom, left and right-hand side of the page.

Font

Try to stay above 10-point text, but less than 14-point. If possible, select a commonly used font such as Times New Roman, Garamond, Arial, or Calibri.

Proof for Spelling, Grammar, and Punctuation

Before you submit your resume, cover letter, and application to a perspective employer, make sure you have gone over it with a fine-toothed comb. This means read and review any potential submissions several times before submitting so that you know there are no errors. We recommend that you have a friend or family member also review your resume and any other parts of your application prior to submission. One of the key functions of a resume is to land you that all-important interview! Let's not derail that mission with any unnecessary errors.

Do not rely solely upon spellcheck to catch potential errors and other grammatical pitfalls. Most word-processing software doesn't know the difference between "their" and "there." So there! Practice a little due-diligence up front, and it will pay off down the road. Also, if your software underlines a word, check it. Computers don't catch everything. Free resources, such as Grammarly and ProWritingAid, could also be useful. If you are a "night stocker" at a local store, but on your resume, you type "night stalker," the computer will not notify you about this typo. If people are not calling you for a job interview, there may be a reason – they may think you are a "night stalker." You don't want that! So, again, carefully review your resume several times and, if possible, have a professional review it, as well.

Keywords

As we referenced earlier in the chapter, computer technology has changed how resumes are discovered by human resources and recruiters. Today, resumes are submitted and stored electronically in large databases called Applicant Tracking Systems (ATS). Employers use "Boolean technology" to find appropriate candidates. Boolean technology is a keyword-based search method, similar to conducting a search on the internet. Because of this type of search method, it is important to use keywords in your resume. For example, if you are seeking a job in pharmaceutical sales, the words "pharmaceutical sales" should be found somewhere in your resume. Keywords can be carefully added to the "Summary of Qualifications" section at the top of your resume.

Length / Number of Pages

Remember, space is valuable on a resume. Similar to other forms of written promotion or advertising, you will need to use your space wisely. The sole purpose of your resume is to interest an employer in your candidacy enough to get you to an interview. Just as it takes a required number of yards for a football player to score a touchdown, a good resume can carry your candidacy into the end zone. The length of your resume is important, but not as important as the content.

The length of your resume will depend upon your years of experience. Rule of thumb is generally 10 years of experience per page. Try to keep your resume to one or two pages if possible. If your experience from more than ten years ago is not relevant, leave it off. Remember this is a tool to sell you and your abilities, not a historical document of your entire career.

If it takes three pages to list all of your accomplishments, then do it! However, don't list three pages of job duties and make it read like a job description. Remember, this document is about you and your specific accomplishments!

Saving Your Resume

When saving your resume as a document on your computer, remember that employers can see how you title your document. It is best to give a name and date, such as john.doe_resume_4.2.2020. Leave off other words (i.e., revised or updated or professional). While these words will help you organize the resumes on your computer, they could be distracting and could potentially make you look like you hop from job to job.

Components of a Resume

Every resume should have a few key parts to it. Here, we will outline what is essential to have on a winning resume.

Contact Information

In the top and center of your resume, write your first, middle (optional), and last name, followed by your physical address, city, state, and zip code. Include your email address and phone number. If any of this information is missing, you may not be contacted, as most databases require complete information for contacting purposes. If you don't put your phone number or email address, an employer cannot reach you. It's amazing how many resumes we view without complete contact information.

Make sure you add a personal e-mail address *that you check regularly.* Don't use an email address that you have through your current employer. It is unprofessional and often not secure. If your email address does not sound professional or might need further explanation during an interview (i.e., hotmama@xxx.com), think about changing it. Your contact information should always be appropriate and up-to-date.

Whatever phone number you put on your resume, make sure to check the voicemail often. There is nothing worse than not responding quickly to a potential employer. In addition, make sure your voicemail is not full on your cell phone. On many cell phones, a full deleted folder can cause issues with the ability to leave a voicemail. Clear out your deleted folder, if possible. Having a full voicemail will make you look unorganized to a potential employer, and they simply may not call you again.

Remember that it is important to *always* display a professional image. Listen to the outgoing message on your voicemail to make sure it is appropriate for an employer to hear. Be careful with the music you select on the call tunes or hold music of your cell phone; songs such as "Take This Job and Shove It," may not help you get that job of your dreams.

Adding a link to your personal LinkedIn profile page has become acceptable. If you do this, make sure your profile looks professional and reflects the details and dates of employment on your resume.

Photos

Photos are becoming more widely used on resumes. However, at the time this book was published, some people still advise against it. Some companies are concerned about the potential for unconscious bias and they have implemented policies to create bias-free recruitment. While this may be a concern, most experts are still encouraging candidates to incorporate a link at the top of their resume to their LinkedIn profile. If you feel your professional appearance is an asset, then adding a link to your LinkedIn profile might be the best way to showcase this to an employer.

Be aware that there are some companies that request that you do not send photos. For this situation, consider having two different resumes, one with a photo and one without.

Summary of Qualifications

We recommend using a "Summary of Qualifications" instead of an Objective Statement on your resume. The main reason is that an Objective Statement is about what *you* want, while a Summary of Qualifications is about how you can meet the *employer's* wants or needs. The Summary of Qualifications is a sales statement about you, your experience and your abilities – what you bring that is valuable to a company.

An example might be:

> **Results-Driven Professional** with expertise in relationship building and territory management. Particular strengths include excellent oral and written communication, communicating product knowledge, providing impeccable follow-up, and a commitment to delivering superior service. Analytical, meticulous, detail-oriented, problem-solver with excellent time management and organization skills. Strong

record of managing projects and improving work processes. Seeking a position in....

Remember, you are selling a product on your resume – and the product is *you*!

Utilizing a Summary of Qualifications sells your skills to an employer. If you are looking for an entry-level position or attempting to switch careers, it may be beneficial to add a statement about what type of position you are seeking to the end of your Summary of Qualifications. By doing this, you will help the reader understand your career objectives and also add important keywords to your resume. An example of this might be simply adding a statement that says, "Seeking a position in …"

A professional resume writer may be able to assist you by putting together your key skills and abilities in a marketable format.

Experience/Dates of Employment

After the Summary of Qualifications section on your resume, include your past work experience. Include titles and dates, and list these in chronological order – most recent goes first! Make sure your dates are correct, since these may be verified during a background check by a potential employer. Under each position you have held, provide a short statement about the company you worked for and the job duties you performed. This area does not need to be written like a job description. Instead, describe the role clearly using keywords. As an example, for your resume to later be discovered in a database search for "sales representative," the words "sales representative" would need to be in your resume.

Accomplishments/Awards/Results

Employers are looking for people who have a history of excelling. Achievements five years ago are important but may not have significant weight in their recruitment decision unless you can show recent accomplishments. You have less than ten seconds to catch the interviewer's attention. Therefore, accomplishments should have bullets or be listed in the top portion of the resume. Avoid using complicated, unrealistic language. Be clear and concise about what you have done.

We look at too many resumes that don't answer two critical questions. As recruiters, we want to know (1) what you did in your position, and (2) how well did you do it? If we review a resume and can't quickly answer those questions, then how can our clients? Again, look critically at your resume for content and communication and have others do the same for you. Does it say what you want it to say and does it answer those two critical questions? It's much better to catch issues now than after you've sent out a hundred copies of what you thought was your perfect resume.

Also, skills and achievements should stand out and be able to be noticed with a quick glance. As we mentioned, bullets are great to grab someone's attention, so save the use of bullets for your accomplishments. Start sentences with action words such as: implemented, selected, achieved, completed, generated, analyzed, administered, etc. Select strong keywords, concrete nouns, and positive modifiers for emphasis.

If you are in sales, your sales numbers are the most important area of your resume. Highlight your past sales accomplishments by including your ranking, past quota attainment, percentage of market share, and/or percentage of plan attainment. Employers see past success as an indicator of future success. Remember to showcase your success by selling yourself. Again, the reader is looking for how well you performed your task.

By adding bullets to your resume that highlight your accomplishments, you will catch the eye of most managers. As an example, a sales manager will view your resume and make a determination of your sales abilities in a matter of seconds. Remember, you have only those few moments to make your impression. By adding bullets of rankings, quota attainments, and awards, you can quickly show your selling abilities, which helps make your case about why you should be interviewed and ultimately hired.

Highlighting your achievements is also important in non-sales positions. Again, the employer should be able to see your accomplishments by just glancing at your resume. Don't hide accomplishments on the second page. Instead, place accomplishments, if possible, on the first page and highlight your successes.

Candidates are plentiful in today's market. What will make you stand out among your competition? The major goal of resume creation is to display your aptitude, ability, and ambition. A strong part of that is showing the skill sets that you've generated along your career path so far. Showcase your skills!

Education

If you feel like your education is the most important component of your background, include it first. Some resumes list Education under the Work Experience section, while others put it before Work Experience. It's your call.

Listing advanced degrees or additional certifications may be very important in certain disciplines. In fact, employers may require certain educational backgrounds. For instance, some positions require a science degree to represent analytic products.

Skills/Training/Certifications

List any relevant training, skills, or certifications in a specific section of your resume. If you have novel skills or training relevant to a particular type of position, make sure you cite them and include their relevance. For instance, if you are applying for an operations management type role and you have an advanced education degree or certification, such as an MBA or CPA, you need to mention these credentials along with any associated accolades. Another example might be a nurse applying for a medical sales role. A nurse has significant comprehensive knowledge within the healthcare and medical field. This could be a huge benefit for an employer within the medical field and one would be remiss to not promote that background. Many nurses are great communicators, too. It could be a perfect fit of background and skill.

Employers love to base hiring decisions upon on quantifiable, objective reasoning. Education and training within a discipline is one way they can accomplish this task. Displaying the background, skill sets, and education that aligns neatly with the job description can be a very strong benefit for your candidacy. This is called "screening for functionality," and it is an important aspect in hiring the right person for the job. Employers are seeking people that can easily function in the position. In *HIRE with FIRE*, we used the acronym "FIRE" to guide employers in hiring the right person; the "F" represented "functionality" in the acronym. Functionality makes up one of the main components of a successful hire. If the candidate cannot function in a position, they are not the best person for the job. Although not a job description, a well-written resume will show the employer how well you functioned in jobs you have held.

References

If you have written references, you can offer them to the interviewer when you meet with them. If you don't have written references but individuals have agreed to speak on your behalf, create a separate document that looks similar to your resume to share these contacts with your interviewer.

To create this document, keep your name, address, and other personal information listed at the top of the document (identical to how you have it on your resume). Then, add the names of your references, their contact information, their relationship to you, and how many years you have known them.

The following is an example of how to set up your reference page.

Example Reference Page:

First Name Last Name
Address, City, State, Zip Code
Phone Number
Email address

References

First Name Last Name
City, State, Zip Code
Relationship: Supervisor, XYZ Company
Years Known: 5

First Name Last Name
City, State, Zip Code
Relationship: Supervisor, XYZ Company
Years Known: 5

First Name Last Name
City, State, Zip Code
Relationship: Supervisor, XYZ Company
Years Known: 5

It is also acceptable to just add a statement to the bottom of your resume such as, "References Available Upon Request." However, if you do this, make sure you have some written references should you be asked to provide them at a later time.

Selecting who to use as a reference can be tricky. Although you may think your neighbor or friend will give you a good reference, they may not. Companies are generally not looking for personal contacts; they want to speak with your professional contacts, past supervisors, customers, or coworkers.

Always ask someone if they would be willing to be your reference. And if you are aware that a reference is going to be contacted, reach out to your reference to let them know. The additional phone call may make all the difference in the urgency of their response.

Willingness to Travel or Relocate

If you are open to travel or relocation, adding a statement to the bottom of your resume such as, "Willing to Travel" or "Willing to Relocate" is also appropriate. During the hiring process, the employer might ask deeper questions relative to the amount of travel and the geography you are willing to cover. Your ability to travel and/or relocate for a position may be an important consideration for a prospective employer. Some individuals enjoy travel within a large area. Others may not mind a relocation. Some candidates will only consider opportunities in their immediate area. If the possibilities of travel or relocation fit your current lifestyle, make sure the interviewer is aware of these flexibilities.

Reason for Leaving Past Employment

If you have had more than three jobs in five years, you can explain your reason for leaving these positions on your resume with a short statement (i.e., downsized, company restructuring, personal leave due to illness). This statement is typically placed on a separate line between the title of your position and the company description on your resume. It is often used for job tenures of less than one year.

Avoid statements about taking a sabbatical to travel. Employers are seeking candidates interested in working hard to achieve their objectives; if you note on your resume that you took a "yearlong sabbatical to see the world," the employer may think you do not need to work.

Other Personal Information

Avoid personal information, such as social security numbers, date of birth, marital status, race, or number of children, for example. This information is not necessary and typically not wanted by employers in the United States.

Omit hobbies and interests unless specific to the job for which you are applying. Avoid listing your salary requirements unless requested by the employer.

You may want to include some volunteer activity. If you volunteer often, pick and choose a few organizations to include that demonstrate your civic motivation or interest in another noteworthy cause. However, you don't want your volunteer work to overshadow your great work experience.

When including volunteerism on your resume, keep in mind that some political or social groups may be polarizing. If the employer disagrees with your viewpoints, it could affect your candidacy. For example, if you were a member of a fraternity in college and the interviewer was in the opposing fraternity, they might not favor you as a candidate.

Honesty

Most importantly, be honest. Background checks are still performed by most employers today. It is very important for employment dates and education to be accurate. Even if an employer extends an offer of employment to you, it may be contingent upon a successful background check or drug screening. If your past employment, education, or screening cannot be verified, you may not be hired or may immediately be terminated.

Include recent jobs, at minimum your last three to four jobs, on your resume. If you have worked for a company and received a paycheck, then that company will show up on a background check. Don't try to hide it from an employer.

Once you have developed your brand, you will be able to sell yourself better in an interview. It's all in the preparation. President Abraham Lincoln (often called "Honest Abe") said it best: "If I had eight hours to chop down a tree, I'd spend six sharpening my ax."[1] Spend time sharpening your resume!

Applications and the Importance of Follow-up

After going through all the work of applying for a position, whether online or in-person, we recommend you follow-up with the company within three to five business days. This extra call will alert them to your resume and lets them know you *want* the position. For candidates that are shy, this can be a difficult phone call to make, but this extra step will show your desire and may make the difference in you getting the position over someone else.

I remember my brother-in-law, Scott, telling us a story from his collegiate years. He needed to fund his education, so he began looking at the best

---

[1] https://www.quotes.net/quote/2442, Quotes-The Web's Largest Resource for Famous Quotes & Sayings, Accessed 4/22/20

positions around for college students. After looking at several different organizations and positions, he decided he wanted to work for a well-known retail supermarket chain. These clerk positions were flexible and compensated college students very well. He filled out the application and heard nothing back. He had visited with some other applicants and found out that the individuals that finally received offers were those that followed up every week and filled out another application. That was the protocol for that organization at that time. Although somewhat unorthodox, Scott had found out how to continually apply and remind them of his candidacy. Well, you can probably guess that his diligence paid off. His follow-up notes, multiple visits, and updated applications resulted in an offer from the company.

We hear similar stories often. I visited with one candidate recently who left a handwritten thank-you note with the hotel desk to give to the interviewer. The interviewer thought this was a great gesture, especially when it was supplemented by the candidate sending an additional thank-you email.

Following up is not easy, but generally we all expect it and appreciate the effort. Yes, there are some companies that tell you not to follow-up on your application, but most will understand people that go out of their way to do so.

The call can be simple. For example, "Hi, my name is _____. I applied for the position of _____. I am very interested in this opportunity and wanted to verify that you have received my information." Then politely ask if there is any additional information that they might need.

Now that we have discussed how to develop your personal brand, let's talk about how to prepare for interviews. It starts with something your mother or father may have told you in high school: "Do Your Homework."

♦ CHAPTER TWO

Step 2 – The E in DESIRE: Educate Yourself about the Opportunity

There are a number of ways you can let a company know you are interested. One way is to understand more about their business before you interview. In other words, do your homework!

Man, it's been years since I heard that one! I remember my mom yelling it into my bedroom when I was a teenager. She never could understand how I could listen to music and study at the same time. But I was a multi-tasker, and you probably are too! Don't forget to multitask when preparing for your next interview. Many candidates will spend hours developing their personal brand (resume, cover letter, and support documents), but then fall short when it comes to interview preparation.

Doing Your Homework

Before interviewing, make sure you understand the company's organization inside and out. This includes a thorough review of the company's website, including their products or services. Be aware of their competition and the overall state of their market. Are they marketing a specialty or commodity type product? If it's more of a commodity type product, think about how they differentiate their product from the competition, and be prepared to discuss this in the interview. If it is a specialty product, show your enthusiasm about the benefits of their product over the competition. This will demonstrate your interview preparation and your interest in helping their business grow. By reflecting upon places you have worked or products and services you have represented in the past, you can compare the similarities and come up with statements that exhibit your ability to use your transferable skills.

Your research should include at a minimum:

- Competitors
- Type of company (public/private)
- Annual sales
- Products and/or services
- Size of the organization
- Their mission
- Leadership team

You may be thinking by now that this doesn't apply to you. You are interviewing for a non-sales type of role. True, you may not be literally selling a company's products or services, but in some facet, you will be representing them. In today's competitive marketplace, virtually every employee within an organization is responsible – directly or indirectly – to that organization's end user or customer. It's now every employee's business to promote the company's brand and contribute to their growth. Engaged employees help produce satisfied customers that help grow the business, along with bringing new opportunities. In every capacity within a company, employers today are seeking individuals who can effectively communicate with their customer base, whether this is an individual in IT, distribution, customer service, or sales. Every employee is a stakeholder in helping a business provide a better customer experience.

As an employee, you have internal and external customers. For example, maybe you are a human resource manager and only deal with employees. This means you work with internal customers. The employee who comes to you for issues with payroll or their time card is your internal customer. You will also have external customers. The services you provide or the products you produce impact someone somewhere. Knowing the *someone* and *somewhere* is important when interviewing. Researching individuals that work for the company and knowing the locations the company serves are details that could easily set you apart from other qualified candidates.

Our discussion thus far has centered around a candidate caring about the company where they may soon work. It seems counterintuitive, but we have to go down this road based upon our experiences in recruiting. Too many times we hear some clients after an interview comment that a candidate simply "doesn't understand our business," or the candidate was "not engaged," or even worse, "they didn't seem to care." You can only imagine the thoughts of an interviewer in these scenarios. They'll probably think, "If a candidate comes across with this attitude in any part of the interview, how are they going to fit in and work for us?"

Companies are looking for loyal employees that will go the extra mile. Show them you have this tenacity by spending time before your interview learning more about what they do!

No matter what type of position you are interviewing for – sales, service, human resources, or other position – you should know everything you can about your potential new employer. Review their website, do a search online, and read reviews from former employees. You may be surprised at how much information is out there in the public domain. This information is valuable and will give you more insight. This insight will allow you to ask deeper questions during the interview process. It will also help you avoid working for the wrong company. If it is a large organization with several divisions, make sure you understand the exact products or services you could

THE E IN DESIRE

represent. It is embarrassing to do significant homework, only to find out you've reviewed the wrong job duties, products, or services!

Research the Interviewer(s)

Once you have researched the company, you may also want to spend some time researching the person (or people) that will be interviewing you. By viewing their profile on LinkedIn, you will be able to see their past experience and education. Gaining this insight might give you a conversation starter when you interview with them. Perhaps you have some of the same connections, root for the same sports teams, or share a hobby. Whatever the connection, developing an early rapport may be very helpful in your candidacy.

Well Thought-Out Questions

Communication is important at all levels during the interview process. Just as the interviewer has prepared and is ready to ask you relevant questions, you need to also prepare a list of three to five questions that will help you understand more about the job and your responsibilities. So, on the first interview bring your arsenal of initial good questions regarding the position (i.e., duties, responsibilities, potential for advancement). Be prepared for follow-up questions from your interviewer.

Throughout the interview process, you will be in what we call the "discovery mode." Just like a lawyer uses discovery to obtain evidence about a case, you are seeking to discover more about this potential employer. Remember discovery is a mutual give and take process – the interviewer wants to know things about you, and you want to know things about the job. To do this, you will need to avoid surface interviewing.

What do we mean? *Surface interviewing* means the interviewee and interviewer don't fully "dive in" with questioning each other. You meet the interviewer; they seem nice, and you never get around to fully understanding more about the job, the company or the organization's culture. As recruiters, we see this frequently when candidates don't fully prepare for interviews ahead of time.

Think about yourself in the position. What challenges would you face? What would the duties be? After giving it some thought, develop three to five deeper questions to ask the interviewer. By doing this, you will gain important information that will help you decide if you *want* the job. Additionally, you will appear more engaged, interested, and enthusiastic to the interviewer. If you need a copy of the job description, ask for it ahead of the interview.

The first interview allows you to establish a bond or rapport with the interviewer early, such as discussing your favorite sports team or industry friends. But after that initial interview, you will need to dive in with questions. Once the discussion about the position begins, go deeper into listening and answering questions from your interviewer. Ask questions for clarity and understanding. You really need to understand their needs and expectations relative to their opening. Stay focused upon the opportunity and keep personal questions early in the interview to a minimum. In fact, avoid getting too familiar this early. Maintain a friendly, yet professional distance. You're not best buddies, yet.

Consider asking questions that allow you to see how this potential employer would handle a situation, or how you would fit into their organization. Learn more about the organization's goals. Again, just like a lawyer preparing for a big case, your goal is to discover all you can about the other party *before* you work for them, not afterward. You can do this by asking well thought-out questions that go beyond the surface. We discussed this in *HIRE with FIRE* and encouraged hiring managers to dive deeper into questioning candidates. But it's a two-way street. Open communication is truly the only way to know if a good employment match can exist.

I've heard many candidates say, "I've sent out more than a hundred resumes." I always want to ask, "Why?" If there truly were one hundred legitimate openings, that's great. But most of the time these candidates have blindly sent resumes to simply anyone and anywhere. Doesn't it make sense to research and come up with a "target list" of companies where you might actually want to work? Spend your high level of detail, follow-up, and focus on companies where you really see yourself working. With the appropriate research and preparation, you can make a huge difference in your visibility and credibility with a prospective company.

By the second interview, create questions that go even deeper into the company's products or services. By developing strong questions, you will set yourself apart from the competition. Employers want to know that you understand their business and that you have researched their company. Below are some examples of these types of questions:

- What are your expectations for the person that fills this position?
- Which of my talents do you feel could be useful in this position?
- What is the structure of the organization above and below you?
- What strategy does the company have for growth?
- How does management view the staff?
- Where do you see the position leading?

Asking and receiving good questions are both important components of the interview process. As an interviewee, it's your responsibility to also engage the interviewer so that they develop enough interest in you to ask you good, tough questions. In fact, they may have just interviewed a candidate right before you that knocked it out of the park. Now, you may have to use your interviewing and sales skills to pull out questions. If the interviewer is not asking you questions, create a dialogue by asking your own questions. You don't want a courtesy interview; you want the full unabridged version.

On occasion, during our post interview follow up, we'll hear from the candidate that they felt they did very well and that the interview was a success. At that point, we want to hear additional details. Did the interviewer ask tough questions indicating a sincere interest in the candidate? Was the interviewer engaged in asking questions about multiple areas of the candidate's experience and background? A quick, friendly, unengaged interview serves no purpose to either party.

Conversely, some candidates will feel they performed poorly on an interview due to a perceived push back of tough questions from the interviewer. They can be wrong. An interviewer asking tough, direct questions may be showing their extreme interest in a candidate. In their mind, they see the potential of this candidate and want to know specifics into how they may respond if given the role. So, if you walk away from an interview and feel like you were mildly interrogated, your candidacy may be firmly intact. You engaged the interviewer, and you may just get the job!

After taking time to learn about a potential employer, you should be able to easily answer the question, "Why do you want to work for this company?" This question is one of the most frequently asked interview questions and often candidates stumble around trying to find a good answer. You can't get excited about something you don't know anything about!

An hour or two spent researching a company can make all the difference relative to working for the right or wrong company. It will enable you to ask well thought-out questions to determine if this is the right career move. It will also show the employer that you are detail-oriented, educated, and interested.

Top Five Reasons You Are the Best Person for the Job

Now that you have spent time researching the company and the people who will be interviewing you, take time to write down the top five reasons that you feel you are the best person for the job.

If you have done your research, you should know about the products or services the company offers. After researching the interviewer and their background, you might be able to connect with them more. Maybe you already work in a position where the customer base is the same, or maybe your education allows you to bring certain skills to the position. Whatever makes you stand out to the interviewer, discuss these traits as a benefit to the employer. For an example, if you were a pharmaceutical salesperson selling a cardiovascular drug and you are now interviewing with a cardiovascular device company, you might want to mention that you know the top cardiologists in the region. Never make the assumption that the interviewer understands your background and skills. It would be sad if you got nervous and forgot to mention such a key benefit in hiring you.

To develop these questions, ask yourself: What do I bring to the company that makes me unique? What skills do I have that will benefit this company? How can I increase their bottom-line or make their organization better? It doesn't matter what position you are seeking—your role as an employee should be to help the company grow. How will you do that?

Interviewers ask many questions during the interview. During this time, it is good to bring up your top five reasons you are the best person for the job. Many have been known to specifically ask the question, "Why should we hire you?" By confidently discussing the top five reasons why you are the best person for the job, you will be perceived as being very prepared. You will show the interviewer that you are engaged and truly *want* the position. The question of why you are the best person for the job is crucial; don't fumble your answer. If you don't know why you are the best person for the position, how would they ever know? Preparing this information ahead of time will help you be more confident during the interview.

Generally, the interviewer will quiz you from an organized bank of questions. In our book, *HIRE with FIRE*, Randy and I are recognized as having one of the premier methods that many employers use. Anticipating areas of questioning is important in interviewing. Similar to studying for an exam, it will help you relax and may make the event more enjoyable.

In *HIRE with FIRE*, we used the acronym, "FIRE," which represents four key traits that many interviewers specifically look for in their successful candidates. These excerpts are not all-inclusive, but that being said, this brief explanation should give you a unique and valuable insight into the mind of a hiring manager during an interview:

Functionality: Does the candidate have the core components for the position? This may include previous experience and education. Does the candidate's experience and background generally align with the job description?

Integrity: This is the personal credo or mantra of the candidate. It may include judgment, honesty, and character-type assessments made by the interviewer.

Results: A candidate should be able to present, verify, and document their past performance.

Enthusiasm: This is demonstrated in the excitement, passion, and interest in the interview and the opportunity. Is the candidate highly engaged?

Following your research on the company and your interviewer, you are one step closer to being ready to interview. Let's talk more now about the actual interview and how to sell your skills to an employer.

Features Tell and Benefits Sell

An interview offers you and the employer an opportunity to exchange information, meet one another, and come to a conclusion about whether the job is right for you. In most companies, candidates go through what is called the "hiring process." The hiring process involves multiple types of interviews. While you could be hired based on one interview with a company, the average is typically three to four interviews, often with multiple interviewers, such as human resources personnel, managers, or prospective peers.

Each type of interview (phone, face-to-face, video, or spending the day with peers/interns) requires a different strategy in order to win. However, one strategy in particular can help you to continue interviewing and be one step closer to winning the job – learning how to sell your skills and abilities to an employer.

During your meeting, provide your interviewer with details about how you will fit within the organization. Discuss specific roles and how you see yourself completing designated tasks. This puts a mental image in the interviewer's mind of you in the position.

Using your abilities to "assume the close" is certainly in order. To assume the close, place the interviewer in a scenario where they picture you working alongside them. An example of this might be, "When I work for you at XYZ Corp., I will …" This statement will accomplish two objectives. First, you will have effectively attempted to close the deal by assuming you will get the job at XYZ Corp., and secondly, you have told the interviewer how you will accomplish a certain task. By doing this, the interviewer will begin to see you in the role, and you will be a step closer to getting the job.

We've used the term, "close" several times throughout this book, so let's look at it more closely. In society, sometimes "close" has a negative connotation, potentially associated with a high-pressure sales environment.

Although used in sales scenarios, it's not negative. In fact, it's natural. For our purposes, it means we've brought a part of our interview process to fruition. For instance, you might have completed the phone interview, then asked for the face-to-face interview, and ultimately asked for the job. Each time we ask for the next step, this is a form of a close. It may go something like, "Based upon my education, experience, and the interview today, will you be moving me on to the next step in the process?" It may feel uncomfortable for some, but asking about the next step and closing along the way has been proven successful relative to getting an interview or successfully landing the job.

If you have a background in sales, presenting yourself may be reminiscent of past sales training where you may recall the adage that "features tell" and "benefits sell." This will be critical to your success in the process since other prospects may be "telling" the interviewer about themselves versus you "selling" the interviewer on how your qualifications or "features" will "benefit" their organization.

To prove your stellar worth to an organization, provide one or more examples of your proven successes and then connect these directly to the position or company. You are then demonstrating the benefit of hiring you! How do you do this? Use a connecting phrase like "which means" or "I will be able to …" To make a maximum impact, you will need to connect a benefit directly back to your feature.

An example might be, "When I was at Acme Car Rental, I was able to use my relationships with several area organizations to promote the Acme brand, *which means* by developing and using similar area and industry relationships within your industry, I believe I can achieve the same successes and achieve another President's Club victory." By doing this, you are connecting your past positive performance – the feature – to a positive future outcome relative to the interviewer's company – the benefit. It's generally agreed that there is a correlation of past performance being indicative of future results, so use this in your favor when interviewing.

As another example, a response to an interview question might be, "I have great relationships with the decision-makers that I have called upon in the past." However, a more thought-out response might be, "I have great relationships with the decision-makers that I have called upon in the past (feature statement), *which means* I feel I can quickly impact the territory and increase the sales of your product within thirty days (benefit statement)." This transition from feature to benefit clearly sets you apart from the other candidates.

This selling technique is not just used by sales professionals. Anyone can use it to sell the skills you offer and how those skills will benefit the employer. As an example, a fast-food worker may be able to describe their experience the same way: "I was able to produce 100 hamburgers per hour when I worked at XYZ Restaurant, *which means* I will be able to easily produce that amount for your business as well."

Remember, presenting yourself for employment is not unlike planning the logistics of delivering any other high-quality product. For simplicity, you (the product) are of the highest quality and bring the features and benefits of any such high-quality item to the interview. But there are other high-quality products in the marketplace, too. This begs the question, "How do I set myself apart from the other high quality 'products' that the customer (interviewer) will see on the day of the interview?" The answer lies in your attitude, accomplishments, and most importantly, your ability to sell yourself.

Now that we have talked about how to sell your skills, let's discuss how to show-up and shine.

♦ CHAPTER THREE

Step 3 – The S in DESIRE: Show Up & Shine

Wow! Can you believe that showing up would be considered one of our tips? Yes, by just showing up, you might get the job. Would it surprise you to know that many times candidates just don't show up for interviews?

According to an article in USA Today, "A growing number are 'ghosting' their jobs: blowing off scheduled job interviews, accepting offers but not showing up the first day and even vanishing from existing positions – all without giving notice."[2] The article goes on to say, "While no one formally tracks such antics, many businesses report that 20 to 50 percent of job applicants and workers are pulling no-shows in some form, forcing many firms to modify their hiring practices."

So, as you can see by these numbers, just showing up is half the battle. Now, let's talk about how to shine.

Your Professional Image

Do you have "the professional look?" If not, how do you get it? Think about these important questions.

- Do you own a business suit and tie? Is it up-to-date?
- Does your make-up or nail polish detract from your appearance?
- Consider the company and job. Do you need to remove or cover up any body jewelry or tattoos?

These are just a few of the questions that only your mother will ask you. However, if you can't tell if your image is professional or not, ask a coworker or mentor. Dressing for success isn't just a phrase. Your attire and your appearance matter to employers. You are representing their brand, not yours.

What Should You Wear to the Interview?

Almost every person will interview at some point in their life. Interviews are not only used to gain employment; they're also used in journalism and other meetings between parties needing consulting or information. For our purposes, it is a formal way to gain a general understanding between two parties in the employment process. Because of the formality, employment interviews require you to dress and groom for the occasion.

The first impression is a lasting one. When you walk in the room, the interviewer will form an opinion of you through nonverbal visual cues.

---

[2] Davidson, Paul, 7-19-18 USA Today, *Workers are 'ghosting' interviews, blowing off work in a strong job market* https://www.usatoday.com/story/money/2018/07/19/strong-job-market-candidates-ghosting-interviews-offers/794264002/ Assessed on 3/19/20

Therefore, wardrobe is very important.

For any professional interview, men and women should wear a conservative two-piece business suit, preferably dark blue or gray. In addition to this, a conservative white or pastel colored long-sleeve shirt or blouse and clean, well-polished dark dress shoes are best. Open-toed shoes are not considered formal and should not be worn in an interview. Men's neckties should be with a conservative pattern. When in doubt, be professional and conservative.

You are selling yourself. It is important to be well-groomed. If you feel you need a haircut, you probably do.

Monitor Other Areas of Life

In addition to your physical appearance, your online appearance also matters. Beware of your image on social networking sites that are open for public search. Google your name to see what may be found about yourself.

Join professional social networking sites. Getting a free account on www.linkedin.com can also be very helpful. LinkedIn is a social networking site for business professionals. Ask your past managers, coworkers, or clients to give you a recommendation, and add this to your profile.

Let's discuss the various types of interviews and some important tips to keep in mind as you progress through the interview process.

Phone Interviews

Typically, most companies start the interview process by doing a phone interview with a human resources manager or a recruiter. Often, that is followed by a second phone interview with the hiring manager.

Because of this, a phone interview is your first chance to make a good impression. Never assume that because the interview is with a human resources manager or a company recruiter that it is not important. These individuals are tasked with prescreening candidates for important skill sets. They are skilled at "weeding out" unqualified candidates.

Phone interviews are as important as face-to-face interviews – maybe even more important. A poor phone interview may certainly end your candidacy. Because of this, they should be taken seriously and given the attention they deserve.

Phone interviews can be challenging at times. When visual communication is lacking, both the interviewer and the interviewee must rely on auditory feedback. This lack of visual communication requires each party to maintain concentration, listen well, and focus.

Have you ever had a conversation by phone with someone that does not respond quickly or offer any audible cues to reassure you that they are listening? It can be frustrating! When I was a nurse, I would have to contact physicians and explain a patient's condition. Most physicians would listen to what I had to say and then quickly respond with doctor's orders on what I was to do next to help the patient. However, a few physicians would take their time in responding. This delay would often be so uncomfortable for me that I would start making my own suggestions. As you can imagine, that didn't always go over very well.

When interviewing, you may also encounter people that pause instead of giving you a reassuring "uh huh" or "I understand." It may be that the interviewer is documenting your answers, and this causes them to pause conversation. There are people that are very analytical; they often listen and take their time to process what you are saying before they respond. Then there are expressive personalities. These are people that quickly give you feedback, such as, "Yes," or "Uh-huh," or "I agree." The expressive personalities make phone interviews easy. You know they understand what you are saying because they offer you constant feedback. Analytical personalities can make phone interviews much more difficult. Their delay in feedback can cause the interviewee (you) to ramble. If you encounter an analytical-type personality, make your answers concise. After giving your answer, simply ask the interviewer if your response fully answered their question.

Although it can be more difficult, a phone interview can still offer you and the employer the opportunity to exchange important information. From the employer's perspective, the phone interview generally determines if you are a reasonable match for the role. And, just as important, it gives you the ability to determine if you have further interest in the position. In this respect, a phone interview offers direction and insight to each party.

Two Types of Phone Interviews

There are two types of phone interviews: unscheduled (the surprise call) and scheduled. Obviously, an unscheduled interview is more difficult because you can be caught off-guard when the interviewer calls. If possible, try to prevent this type of interaction. It's fine to let the interviewer know that you are very happy to hear from them and if possible, you would like to schedule a time to talk so you can be in a quiet place and feel better prepared. Most interviewers will respect this and schedule a time with you. This extra time will help you be well-informed about the company before you interview.

How to Prepare for a Phone Interview

There are a few steps you can take to be fully prepared for a phone interview:

Check your signal and quality of your call. If you have the availability of a landline or good VOIP connection, that might be your best scenario.

Keep your resume updated and close by. It will help you answer questions about your past experiences. In this respect, it can act as an outline to help you maintain your thoughts and direction during the phone call.

Set a place aside that is free of distraction. Background noise can be distracting to you and the interviewer. It can cause a lack of focus which might impact your otherwise great performance. A room behind a closed door can help. If you need to put man's best friend in the backyard, do it. You can celebrate your great interview with "Fluffy" or "Spot" after the call!

Smile during your phone interview. Research has shown that the tone of your voice will come across more pleasant and friendly if you smile while you are talking. Plus, employers just like happy, capable employees. Many studies have validated that a high degree of employee satisfaction creates longer tenure in employees and happy external customers.

Stand up during the phone call. It has also been noted that by standing up during your phone conversation your voice will sound more energetic and enthusiastic. Stretching out your upper torso allows you to have the full strength of your lungs. This will also help you with nervousness and will allow you to show your enthusiasm better.

Listen. Without seeing the other person, it is hard to know when to stop talking. Follow this rule of thumb, when you feel you have answered a question, allow for a moment of silence. This will let the interviewer know that you are through with your answer and they can proceed to the next question. Allow the interviewer to speak without interrupting. Make sure you understand the question fully before giving your answer.

Answer Questions Fully. Answer questions in a clear and concise manner without rambling. Be thorough and stay within the premise of the topic asked.

Be prepared to answer questions about gaps in your resume. It's important to have a prepared response to this inquiry. Gaps happen for various reasons, but an unsubstantiated gap in your resume will need to be explained. This topic will be covered in more detail in Chapter Four.

What Not to Do on a Phone Interview

- Do not drive while participating in a phone interview. The interviewer will feel your distraction. It could also be considered poor judgment. Many companies do not allow usage of cell phones while driving as part of their policies. If you are not able to interview when the manager calls, get the interviewer's name and phone number and a good time to reach them back. This shows the interviewer that you don't want to be distracted during your call with them.
- Do not use a speaker phone.
- Remove earrings if you wear a headset. Earrings can cause a distracting background noise.
- Make sure you are away from noise and distractions (put pets in another room, hire a babysitter if needed, etc.)
- Avoid chewing gum or food. Do not smoke cigarettes.
- If possible, disable call waiting. If not possible, ignore incoming calls.
- Avoid giving out too much personal information (i.e., financial problems, marital status, children, etc.). Don't talk too much!
- Avoid questions about salary and benefits unless brought up by the interviewer. This topic can be handled later in the interview process.

How to Close a Phone Interview

Closing the interview is the most important step of the interview process for any job seeker, especially for a sales professional. Always ask at the end of the interview when the hiring decision is expected to occur. Additionally, inquire into whether you will have a second or third interview. They may not immediately confirm that you will be moving forward, but it shows great initiative to ask. Express your sincere interest in the position to the interviewer. We will discuss ways to close an interview more in-depth in Chapter Six.

Send a Thank-You Note and Follow-up After the Interview

This is one of the most critical areas of showing enthusiasm during the interview process. We will discuss how to write a thank-you note more in Chapter Six.

The Most Important Tip: Show enthusiasm and excitement about the position! Research shows that interviewers often make decisions based on who they "feel" will do the best job. Decisions are not always completely based upon qualifications or past performance. Those aspects are important, but many times it's the perceived drive, interest, and enthusiasm that wins the position. Show them you *want* the job!

Video Interviewing

If you are like most of the population, you hate being on camera. But you received a call from your recruiter or human resource manager asking you to do a GoToMeeting, Zoom, Skype, or FaceTime interview. Now what?

Well, don't panic. You're in good company if you dislike being on camera.

It can be intimidating to have a live conversation, especially with a potential employer. But stop right there! The most important aspect to realize is that they would not be wasting time performing this type of interview if they weren't interested in you! So, relax, sit back, and just prepare.

Video interviewing is becoming much more common. Several of our clients have skipped the traditional phone interview step and their initial screening processes in favor of video formats. As business becomes more and more global and technology becomes more integral to business development, it saves time and money in the interview process for employers to utilize video technology. It's important for job seekers to familiarize themselves with the process of video interviewing to make the decision for employers clear. Here are a few tips to consider:

- **Prepare your computer or phone.** If the employer is requesting to do a video interview, invest in a quality web camera if your laptop is not already equipped. These are typically around $25 to $30 and sold at most office supply stores.

- **Tidy up your surroundings**. Make sure you are in a well-lit area with a professional background. This is not the time to have phones ringing, pets making noise, or any other distractions visible. Before starting the interview, check to make sure the framing of the video is flattering. You want the interviewer to see you from the waist up while also showing the cleanliness and organization of the area around you.

- **Wear an appropriate outfit**. Select a suit or some type of professional dress. Do not dress down just because you are doing a video instead of an in-person interview. Treat video interviewing the same as any other professional interview. It is basically the same as a face-to-face interview, so treat it with the same respect. Dress up completely – no sweatpants or shorts out-of-frame!

- **Look at the camera lens.** It is important to look at the camera and not at the interviewer on your phone or computer screen. Looking at the camera will give the effect that you are creating eye contact while also creating a more flattering perspective for the interviewer.

Also, check to make sure the camera is pointing directly at you to ensure that the interviewer will see you properly.

You may be asked to set up a Skype account if you do not already have one. It is simple to set up an account on Skype's website. After you have done this, you will need to provide the employer with your Skype ID, so pick a professional username. Additionally, you will need to know the interviewer's Skype ID and add them to your approved Skype contact list prior to your phone call.

In most interviews, the employer initiates the phone call to you, instead of you calling them. The same goes for a Zoom, GoToMeeting or FaceTime interview. Although FaceTime takes less time to set up, you will still need to learn how to use it ahead of time. Consider practicing with a friend.

If you are using a camera on your phone to do a video interview, get a stand for it so that your camera is stabilized and not moving or shaking. You don't want to give your interviewer vertigo or make them nauseous or dizzy.

None of this is difficult, but some forethought can take you a long way. Practicing and organizing for your interview will increase your confidence and enhance your performance.

Face to Face Interviews

You've gotten the interview! Hooray! Now it's time to reflect and prepare your talents for your performance. Obviously, the organization that you will be meeting with considers your credentials strong enough to stir their curiosities. Again, they want to talk, and so do you – that's great!

Now that we've celebrated, let's humble ourselves in the fact that this first interview can be a one-time opportunity for a slam-dunk. It's worth mentioning again: the first impression the interviewer makes about you is critical and often lasting. Your diligent thoughts, research, and preparation will be the difference between you and the other candidate(s). Keep in mind that an interview offers you and the employer an opportunity to exchange information, meet one another, and come to a conclusion about whether the job is right for you.

Arriving at Your Interview

If at all possible, arrive for your interview at least ten minutes early. This allows the interviewer to witness your punctuality and creates reason that you will be on time for future work assignments. It also exhibits your excitement and interest in the role. Not to mention, arriving early will provide you a margin of error so that if you have trouble parking, locating the meeting location, or simply finding the person you are to meet, you won't be late.

Meeting the Interviewer(s)

Follow the interviewer's cue on where to sit. Upon meeting the interviewer(s), remember a firm handshake and a smile are always appropriate. An ice-breaker regarding some type of pleasantry may also be beneficial, such as commenting about their new building or decor of the office. The first five minutes usually establishes the outcome of the interview – whether you get to the next round. Try to develop a rapport with the interviewer. A firm handshake at the end of the interview is also important.

Be in the moment. Now comes the importance of the present! You're in the moment, and the present includes your performance during the interview. This is reflected in the way you field questions and handle yourself, both through response and body language.

Body language is also important during the interview. Sitting forward in your chair, yet still being relaxed, shows the interviewer you are interested in hearing all the details. Sit up straight, no slouching allowed. Be attentive and remember to maintain eye contact and smile. Greet your interviewer with enthusiasm without going over the top.

Listen. By all means, listen carefully throughout the interview. So many times, an opportunity is lost due to not listening carefully to a question or comment. It's very easy, particularly if you're nervous, to be thinking about your next question or statement and miss something in the moment. So slow down and listen. Your attentiveness will be noted. There will be time for your next interaction. In fact, we've found that some candidates have been so excited and engaged that they actually interrupt and talk over the interviewer. Not good. Take your time and be respectful, like you would with your best friend telling you about an important life event.

Be friendly, but not too casual, even if the interviewer comes off very "laid back." Beware! They are in the interviewing chair, and this gives them the ability and the right to choose the interview format. You, on the other hand, are their guest and interviewing for your next important career move. Often, interviewers will be informal to encourage you to open up and relax. This can cause a candidate to talk too much and offer irrelevant information. Err on the side of formality, and be strategic with your answers. Listen closely so that you may anticipate the next question.

Avoid rambling. Answer questions directly and completely, but try and be concise. Randy is always talking about this with his candidates. He is an amiable-expressive personality type, so he likes to talk. He readily admits to that! It's not necessarily a bad thing. In fact, knowledge of that part of your personality is great because you'll know you need to "reel it in" during the interview. On the flip side, if you're more of the analytic or quiet type, be aware that you may need to plan your dialogue a bit more. A little down time in the interview is okay, but too much dead air time might lead to the interviewer having some concerns over your ability to communicate effectively.

Avoid negative comments. No matter your personality type, avoid negative comments, particularly directed at current or past employers. As an important reminder, smile often and talk enough. You should stick to the business at hand; there is no need to volunteer unnecessary personal information. At this point, you are not attempting to be the interviewer's "best buddy." Sure, you want to find common ground, but be cognizant of time and the content of the interview. The interviewer has particular information that he or she wants to review, and you, too, have an agenda to complete. If you find too much common ground and talk about it at length, neither you nor the interviewer will have a good interview. How can that be? Well, the interviewer may have an incomplete view of you as a candidate, and you may not have a complete understanding of the job or company.

As an example, I once had a hiring manager who asked a candidate the question, "Tell me about yourself." The candidate responded by giving important career details but then started talking about her boyfriend who lived in Florida. After hearing this, the manager became hesitant about hiring her for the position because the position was based in New York. He was convinced that she would ultimately move to Florida and not stay with the company long. He had already lost one employee and didn't want to take the chance on losing her too. If she had left out the information about her boyfriend or had further clarified her statement, she probably would have been selected. Too much personal information can be detrimental to your candidacy. Don't offer personal information that is not relevant to the job.

Instead, help the interviewer see all the benefits of bringing you on board, both the personal and the professional attributes.

What to Bring to the Interview

It is important to look organized. Bring a portfolio with at least one copy of your resume for every person you will be meeting. Include a reference page, along with documentation (often called a "brag book") of your past performance, awards, and achievements.

You may also want to bring a professional looking pen and notepad to write down information the interviewer is discussing with you. Be prepared to fill out an application. Bring dates of employment, salary history (if you are open to disclosure and allowable under state law) and references with you. Don't forget to bring your well-thought-out questions and the top five reasons you are the best person for the job.

Most importantly, bring *passion*! This is a critical step in the process of *selling* your skills and abilities to get that job that you *want*. We highlight those two words because you *want* to be at this juncture in the employment process – not because of a recruiter, a family member, a friend, or just because you want to "see what else is out there." You are preparing to interview because you *want* this opportunity and you have earned it. Often, we hear about candidates getting a job offer based upon their *excitement* and *energy*. Whatever you need to do on the morning of the interview to bring your energy level up – caffeine, exercise, listening to your favorite music – do it.

What Not to Bring to the Interview

- Leave your cell phone in the car! It is a distraction – if not to the interviewer, it will be a distraction for you.
- Don't bring your children, relatives or any friend. If you have to ride with someone to get to an interview, leave them outside.
- Don't bring food or beverages into an interview. You might laugh about this one, but I heard a story once of someone that brought an energy bar and started eating it during the interview. Unless you have low blood sugar, I wouldn't recommend it.

Ride-Along, Shadowing, and Other Forms of Evaluation

Apart from the regular face-to-face interview, an organization may ask you to participate in an outside form of evaluation. This activity might be a form of ride-along, job shadowing, or some other project. The purpose of this additional activity is to obtain another view of your abilities and interactions. Some might call this activity "a day in the life." It can be helpful for both the candidate and the employer in that the candidate can get a real-life view of the position and the requirements for the role. From the employer's perspective, they may be determining your ability to interact with outside individuals, as well as potential coworkers.

Generally hosted by an individual that might be your coworker, the day may appear more casual in nature. But it's not casual. It is a part of the formal evaluation process. Beware, it's easy to share too much information, talk too much, or simply make the wrong impression when informality is present. Remember, you are highly interested in the position, and you should maintain a degree of formality. It is very important that you treat this opportunity with the same respect and enthusiasm that you would any other part of the interview.

We once had a candidate do a ride-along with a current employee (a field sales representative) and after their interaction, the employee complained to the manager about the candidate's behavior during the ride-along. It was eye-opening. The employee described how the candidate changed the radio station in their car to another station several times without asking first, adjusted various climate control settings, and talked too much. These actions came across as disrespectful to the employee hosting the ride-along. In this situation, the candidate showed no signs of disrespect during the two face-to-face interviews with the manager, but this event provided insight into how the candidate might eventually interact with coworkers and potentially, customers.

Ride-Alongs

If you are doing a ride-along as a sales representative, the ride-along host is evaluating you in respect to how you meet and greet customers and others. Maintain a friendly, business-like appearance to your host's customers and their office staff.

The ride-along process is definitely a part of your interview, and you are a guest. Generally speaking, the host or evaluator is usually a high performer and an integral part of their staff. They will have important, credible input into your day's activities. It is also helpful to be prepared with a good list of relevant questions for the ride-along. This portrays your interest, enthusiasm, and preparedness for the day's activity. Avoid questions about compensation, vacation, and benefits for now. Those can be directed toward HR when (and if) the time arises. Rather, focus your attention on the current job activities that might be related to high producers in the role, such as, "What have you found that makes you successful and creates more opportunity?" or "What do I need to accomplish to be considered as a top employee?"

If you are in sales, aligning your past sales accolades and accomplishments could be helpful, too. Talking about similar products, sales ideas, and common ground can help you bond with your host and create a favorable impression. Discussing your transferrable skills and the items you learned in previous positions can also be helpful when making a case for your future success with their firm. Remember, they are looking for an addition to their team that can provide solutions to their current situation. Your job is to show them how they can accomplish that result by hiring you!

From this activity, you are gaining an insight into how you might approach the position, the organization, and their workday. Your host is doing the same thing in determining your ability to successfully assume the role. From a more global perspective, they are determining your overall business fit into the position. Did the candidate smile and interact appropriately with customers and others easily? Did they display a strong interpersonal skill set during the day? For instance, is the candidate a good listener, or do they interrupt others? Were they engaged fully in the day? Do they have an abundance of energy without being over the top?

Remember, your discussion with this individual will likely get back to the hiring manager. To be invited by their organization to participate in this activity shows a sincere interest in your candidacy. Throughout the day, be gracious and polite.

Be prepared for a debriefing after the day's activities. This can be a very important part of your day. Your host may have some specific or very general questions to ask. When answering, take your time, and reflect upon the day. Discuss what you learned and what you found of interest. Compliment the host on how they conducted themselves during the interactions and that you appreciated the opportunity to travel with them. Also, you will generally have the opportunity to ask them questions after your day. Keep those questions relevant to the day's activities, and when appropriate, use those answers to further your potential employment. Use the conclusion of the day to close for the next step. Let your host know why you are interested in the role and how the day further interested you in the position.

Job Shadowing and Internships

Job shadowing or an internship is very similar to a ride-along event. Job shadowing is sometimes used internally within an organization, potentially as a form of job enrichment. An organization will move an employee to a different area or task to see if it might be a more fitting or interesting position for them. Additionally, a candidate might be brought in as a part of their interview process to follow an employee for a day or longer to see if the candidate has a sincere interest in that employee's role. This might be looked upon as a trial run, checking the interest level of either a current or future employee. Many times, internships are a collegiate activity set up by a career development office at a college or university. These are generally temporary placements, sometimes for college credit, and/or compensation, to assess the student's interest in a particular career area.

Internships, interviews with peers, shadowing, and ride-along days are all part of the evaluation during the hiring process. You may have requested this meeting to evaluate if you *want* the job, but keep in mind the employer is still evaluating you.

The next chapter discusses how to show your interest and integrity during the interview process.

🔥 CHAPTER FOUR

Step 4 – The I in DESIRE: Interview with Interest and Integrity

Employers are seeking candidates with integrity. To evaluate this attribute, they will use general, situational, and behavioral questions. Each of these lines of questioning will give them a unique look into your thoughts, character, and potential actions as an employee.

Your response right now is most likely, "Well, I answer every question with integrity." While that may be true, it is important to show integrity to employers by answering their questions with honesty in a concise manner that also portrays confidence.

During the interview process, you need to be open about your background with the interviewer. This is not the time to make up information or try to bluff your way through. This happened during an interview with a potential candidate I worked with. When asked if they knew anyone in a certain department in a hospital, they quickly responded, "Yes." Unfortunately, when they were asked who, they were unable to come up with a name. The manager thought this could be a red flag. Although the candidate most likely responded "yes" to the question because they wanted the position, ultimately the manager did not move forward with them because their response was not substantiated.

Let's start by going over some common interview questions. As we discuss these questions, we will offer you strategies to help you also pique the interviewer's interest in you throughout each stage of the interview process.

Answering Common Questions

Let's face it—some questions are hard to answer. If you recently resigned from a position because you didn't get along with your supervisor or a coworker, it might be hard for you to find a positive answer when asked about your reason for leaving your last position. While it is important to answer the question in a positive manner, it is also important to answer an interviewer's questions with honesty and integrity.

Ultimately, the interviewer is attempting to determine if you will be a fit for their organization, and your honesty and candidness are of key interest. For instance, if your last manager had a micromanagement style and you don't work well with this type of manager, it might be important to tell the interviewer that you are "a motivated, self-starter and you are open to coaching, but prefer not to be micromanaged." This highlights your strengths, but allows the interviewer to decide if you would fit within their organization. This is a critical alignment between you and the prospective organization. You want this opportunity to be a fit. If you simply state, "My last boss micromanaged everything I did, and I didn't like it," you will be at a disadvantage.

The goal of an interview is for you and the interviewer to better understand each other and how your skills would fit within their organization. The culture of an organization is important; both you and your future employer should want you to fit into the culture well. No one is perfect, and hopefully your interviewer is open-minded to your flaws and his or her flaws, too. Everyone has the opportunity to be better, and we've all made mistakes. If you've had an instance in your career where you made a misstep and it becomes a discussion point, always point out what you learned so that it is unlikely to reoccur. This shows the benefit of your experience and your honesty.

Here are some of the most commonly asked questions and some suggestions on how to structure your response.

Question 1: "Tell me about yourself."

Interviewers often like to get you talking so they can gather information. Questions like, "Tell me about yourself," are used to help you relax. However, this type of broad questioning can cause a candidate to give too much information about themselves. They're not asking you, "What is the meaning of life," so keep your answers concise and confident. This is a question that you should welcome, since it is common and should be loosely rehearsed. Your content can vary depending on the opportunity, but your key reviewed material will be fairly consistent.

This question might be answered by mentioning:

- something about where you grew up
- where you attended school
- prominent career moves
- maybe a hobby

Then quickly shift to talking about:

- your education
- your career experience and how it relates to the job

Keep your answer focused. Try not to focus your answers about yourself, instead discuss what you have to offer to the company. Give a few precise details about yourself and career, but don't go into great detail about your family, favorite sports team, or that your car doesn't work. Remember, any details you give will create a picture in the interviewer's mind about how you will perform if given the job. If you tell them you just had car trouble, they might assume that you always have car trouble, and therefore, might always be late or not show up. Our minds are often like this; if we don't have a complete picture, we will often fill in the blanks to complete a scenario of a situation.

"Tell me about yourself" is one of the most commonly asked questions, and having an idea of how you will answer it will help you feel more comfortable in the interview. If you notice that you have something in common with the interviewer (i.e., sports, art, etc.) it is fine to bring out this information. But don't exaggerate to create something in common. If you are not into sports, don't act like you are. Be yourself!

What if the interviewer asks you to describe yourself? This question is very similar to "Tell me about yourself," however, the interviewer may be trying to get you to divulge some character traits. To prepare for this question, write down some character traits that make you the best person for the job. Are you a team player? Are you detail-oriented? Do you give over a 100% effort on the job? Use this question to sell your abilities and traits to the employer. If you've taken personality tests that you feel provide a favorable profile for you regarding this position, then talk about that data and why these traits may have helped you become successful.

Question 2: "Why do you want to work for this company?"
If you did your prep work researching the company and the job, you should have an idea of why you are interested in the job. If you are just applying because you are hoping this is a better opportunity, keep researching and make sure this is the right move for you based upon your background and interest. It's imperative that you have a couple of concrete reasons why you are interested so you can effectively communicate this to the interviewer. A good interviewer will quickly spot sincerity and interest from a candidate, and this will reflect on their perception of your integrity.

We once had an interviewer ask a candidate, "Why are you interested in this job?" and the candidate responded by saying, "I need something to motivate me to get out of bed in the morning." Hopefully, you can develop a better answer than this to show your interest in the position! Align your past experiences with what you believe this opportunity may offer. Your successes in your previous positions that correlate to the company's products or services should be highlighted and discussed.

Question 3: "Why are you leaving your current position?"

When answering this question, never offer excuses or be negative about your past employer. You might simply discuss how this new opportunity is a better fit for your skills and career. Focus on what you learned in your previous position and how you will use those transferable skills in your new position. An example statement might be, "I was able to hone my skills in selling products at XYZ Company. I excelled at their training academy and was a high producing representative. Now I'm prepared to market your product. I believe this is a vertical move for me relative to my career, and it looks like an excellent fit."

Always talk positively and relate past employment and skills you acquired to this new opportunity. No one likes to hear an individual bash an employer. Remember, the company where you're interviewing is an employer, and no employer scores 100 percent on employee satisfaction. You may be perceived as "the problem." You can talk about industry challenges and the like, but take the high road on this one. Discuss the good aspects of the previous company, and how you became better in your job and the industry during your tenure.

Question 4: "What are your greatest strengths?"

This is your chance to sell yourself. Your strengths should relate to the position for which you are applying. If you can't immediately come up with a list of your strengths, ask an associate or friend. The people who know you well can be your greatest cheerleaders. Where you may be modest about your abilities, your friends may be able to quickly give you a list of your attributes.

Now that you have your list, think of these strengths before the interview so that you can give the interviewer examples. These could be a strong work ethic, conscientious, reliable, goal-oriented, and trustworthy, for example. Providing examples of your strengths that can be tied directly to the opportunity is key. If attention to detail is one of your strengths, then provide an example such as, "Because of my detailed and documented call history with a previous client, I was able to provide a proposal that exactly met their needs, resulting in a major sale."

Providing your strengths and the corresponding outcomes should be of particular interest to your interviewer. As discussed in a previous chapter, verbiage such as "which means" also connects your strength to the outcome. "I have a strong working knowledge of the industry *which means* I can hit the ground running and gain new clients." Providing your interviewer with some of your strengths is great, but tying those strengths to a benefit for them can take you past the finish line.

Question 5: "What are your greatest weaknesses?"

Answering this question requires integrity. You are still trying to sell yourself, so be cautious about how you discuss your weaknesses. If asked about a particular trait, like if you are usually tardy, then you need to answer the question with an honest assessment of yourself and your time management skills. However, when an interviewer asks what is your greatest weakness and you realize that you are often not on time, a well-thought-out answer can make all the difference in how your weakness is presented. An answer could be constructed like this: "I am a very detail-oriented person and sometimes it makes me run a bit behind. I get so wrapped up in what I am doing that time can get away from me." In giving an answer such as this, you are being honest with yourself and the employer, but you have left them with the idea that you are still an overachiever and particular about your work. Never give a weakness without providing some form of benefit to the potential employer.

Question 6: "Who do you know?"

Professional contacts are important, especially in sales. If you are interviewing for a sales role, you may be asked about your contacts or current client base within their industry. Typical questions might be, "Who do you call upon?" or "How would you leverage your current contacts to sell this product?" If you are asked these questions, use your gut instinct. Don't give out information that you are not comfortable giving out and never say you have relationships with people or departments that you don't actually have. The interviewer could continue to ask you secondary-level questions that you cannot fully answer, making you look disconnected from the industry.

Question 7: "What do you see yourself doing five years from now?"

Be honest with this question. If you don't see yourself in management, then don't give that answer. It is fine to tell the interviewer that you love what you are doing now and want to continue to do it. If you would like to mentor or train other people, then tell the interviewer. Companies want people that work hard and love what they do. Position this answer to indicate career and improved performance progression over time. For instance, "I was a top ranking representative last year within the top 10 percent of the sales force. This year with the development of some of my key accounts, I expect to be in the top 5 percent."

Question 8: "What motivates you to put forth your greatest efforts?"

Interviewers can ask this question in a variety of different forms. They really want to know what motivates you. Are you motivated by your family? Success? What about tangible rewards (i.e., money, bonuses) or intangible rewards (i.e., plaques, trophies, recognition)? This question can also reflect upon your value system and your integrity as an individual. Avoid cliché answers like, "I want to help others." It's not a bad answer; it's simply incomplete. "I want to help others by being on the marketing team of your antibiotic division." That's better, right?

Question 9: "What qualifications do you have that make you qualified for this job?"

This involves comparing your accomplishments relative to the job description. As we mentioned before, make sure you have read a copy of the job description. Understanding the job and its functions will give you incredible insight into what the interviewer wants to know. Your ability to meet the needs of the company and the position, as well as function well within the role, should be apparent to the interviewer.

Hopefully, your qualifications exceed those cited in the description. Simplistically, your accomplishments show what you did and how well you did it. The closer you align your accomplishments to those requirements or needs from your prospective employer, the better. You want to be the most accomplished applicant, so during the interview, ask questions and provide answers that give concrete examples of your abilities and qualifications. At face value, an initial screening may be an exercise in "checking the box," in that the minimum requirements have been met to move your candidacy to the next level. However, the real work will occur in subsequent interviews where you should demonstrate your superior abilities and performances with valid proof sources.

Question 10: "Why should I hire you?"

This popular interview question has been around for years. Answering it correctly requires a deep understanding of four things: the company, its products, the interviewer, and most importantly, you.

It also requires you to make a pitch, just like a salesperson would do to sell a product. As recommended earlier, if you go into the interview with the list you created of the top five reasons why you are the best person for the job, this question should not be difficult to answer. Remember to discuss the reasoning followed by some form of validation. Additionally, present these accomplishments as transferrable skills into their opportunity. You are effectively selling your abilities within their role by developing favorable comparisons between your past accomplishments and their present needs.

Handling Gaps in Your Resume

Be prepared to answer questions if there are any gaps in your resume. Answer the question honestly. If you were laid off or downsized, tell the interviewer how many other people were laid off and if this was the first wave of lay-offs or you were able to make it to the second wave. Offer them references from the employer you were laid off from.

If you took time off for personal or family reasons, tell the situation briefly, move on with the discussion, and avoid details. Simply state that you took time off for personal or family needs, and the issues have been resolved and you are able to be devoted completely to this role, should it be offered to you. Again, the interviewer does not need to know the details of your situation. They only need to know that you can successfully perform the job duties if given the position.

Situational or Behavioral Interview Questions

Situational or behavioral questioning is commonly used by today's interviewers. The situational interview and behavioral interview are based on real work or life situations. An example of a situational interview question might be, "Describe a situation where you have had to deal with a difficult person." Answering a question like this may concern you. What is the correct answer?

Maybe when you read that question, some person immediately came to mind, or maybe a memory that you wish you could forget. We all have people that we feel are difficult, yet we rarely reflect on how that person made us feel and how we overcame the issues or situation. Virtually everyone has encountered issues and potential disagreements when working with coworkers. We all have different backgrounds and experiences. It happens, and it is human nature. No one is perfect. Again, we just want to forget it happened!

By asking this question, the interviewer may be attempting to find out how you handle adversity. Does it break you? Most likely, though, they are evaluating how you work through difficult situations.

Questions that are behavioral in nature are best answered with a four-step process. To answer questions in a clear and concise manner without rambling, describe the circumstance, the task, the action you took, and the result of your action. This format will allow you to remain focused on the question and will help you complete your answers fully.

This technique is called the "STAR method." The basic components of using the STAR format are:
S: *Situation*
T: *Task*
A: *Action*
R: *Result*
According to Allison Doyle, "Behavioral interview questions are questions about how you have behaved in the past. Specifically, they are about how you have handled certain work situations. Employers using this technique to analyze jobs and define the skills and qualities that high-level performers

have exhibited in that job."[3]

Here is an example of how you might answer a situational question by using the STAR method:

> My department was having issues with the billing department. The billing manager of that department did not feel that information from my department was getting to them in a timely manner. Because of this, as the supervisor, I met with this person in an attempt to understand their perspective. I offered to work with them and create a form and procedure to assist their department. By implementing a meeting with this person and trying to understand their concern, I avoided further complaints. The billing manager was happy with the new process. This allowed the billing department to invoice customers quicker and our departments to work better together.

The Situation was that the billing department was having issues getting information in a timely manner. The Task was your role in correcting the situation by creating a form and procedure to get the information to billing faster. The Action was implementing the process. Finally, the Result was that customers were being invoiced quickly and efficiently.

Using the STAR format will help you answer questions with detail while still being concise. And most importantly, the STAR method allows you to give a complete answer while focusing on the positive in the situation. The STAR format works great with questions that begin with "Tell me a time when you had to…" or "Describe a situation when you…"

Strange Situational Questions

There are some interviewers that may like to use a shock approach when interviewing to see how you respond. As an example, the interviewer might ask you, "How would you test a refrigerator?" or "Why is a manhole cover

---

3 Doyle, A. (2020, March 6). How to Use the STAR Interview Response Method. Retrieved from The Balance Careers: https://www.thebalancecareers.com/what-is-the-star-interview-response-technique-2061629.

round instead of square?" According to Lin Grensing-Pophal, in the article, "'If You Could Be Any Vegetable' and Other OffBeat Interview Questions," when employers ask questions that seem strange, they are looking for the candidate's ability to react quickly, think on their feet, and be creative.[4]

When an interviewer offers questions of this nature, don't panic. Do your best to form an answer. It is okay to be humored and let them know you feel the question is not typical. However, use this time to bond with your interviewer and show your abilities to use analytical sound reasoning. Keep in mind that for most of these questions, there is no right or wrong answer. It is simply positioned to assess your wit, mental acuity, and potential creativity. Enjoy the moment. They are not trying to derail your candidacy. While questions like these can be frustrating, take them in stride and realize that your behavior and how you approach answering the question may in fact be what sets you apart from other candidates.

There are two additional ways to set yourself apart from other candidates: Being able to showcase your results (past accomplishments) and having an abundance of enthusiasm. In the next two chapters, we show you how to grab the employer's attention by letting them know you are the best person for the job.

---

[4] Lin Grensing-Pophal, HR Magazine, Spring 2020, *If You Could Be Any Vegetable' and Other OffBeat Interview Questions*, p. 10

♦ CHAPTER FIVE

Step 5 – The R in DESIRE: Results

We all want results when we work hard on something. If you are trying to lose weight, you want the scale to reflect your results. If you have studied for a test, you want a superior test score. Results are important.

It's important to maintain organization and direction when presenting your results to employers. Describe your work experiences and particularly your successes. Be specific in what transpired and the positive outcome that you created. Then, you can explain how these skills are transferable to their environment. For instance, when you've outlined a future action within a 30-60-90 day plan, be detailed about when and how the objective will be met, the parties involved, and the net positive outcome expected for the organization. A 30-60-90 day plan is simply an outline of the first three months of employment. Most upper level managers will be conceptually thinking in a business objective or goal-oriented mindset. This might be meeting a specific monetary growth goal in dollars or an objective product unit production goal. Maybe it's a specific service goal relative to how many patients are seen over a period of time. There are business objectives for all types of organizations, including not-for-profit and government entities. When you are putting together your presentation, make sure your assertions are realistic. As discussed earlier, an understanding of their specific business is helpful. In most industries, you will be able to research a significant amount of information on associated topics in industry and business. If your interviewer has asked you for a presentation, you can query the company about their expectations or talk to others you may know within their industry.

Keep in mind that an employer hires you in order to get results. You are not getting a job just to fill a position. You are being hired to produce something. Maybe you are producing a product or providing a service. Perhaps you will be cutting costs for the company. No matter what will be your directive, you are being hired to get results.

In this chapter, we want to look at your results. What have you produced in your past work experiences? If this is your first job, then what did you produce in high school or college? Were you the president of an organization? Were you a volunteer? Did you raise money for an organization? In other words, what did you do that created value?

Results include both your past and present performance. Showing results is important no matter what type of position you are seeking. For sales positions, it has become common practice to show the interviewer your past sales accomplishments. Often this data will be contained in your "brag book." We'll review the brag book in detail later on in the chapter, but no matter what job you are seeking, it is important for you to take the time to showcase some of the work that you have done, awards you have received, or knowledge you have gained. With proper planning and execution, this will place you a step ahead of other candidates.

Past performance deals with questions of past accomplishments, which may include performance documentation. Instead of a brag book, sometimes interviewers prefer a separate, unbound proof of performance or a digitally scanned version they can easily share with other interviewers.

The potential issue with creating the brag book is that it may be tempting to reference it too often during the interview. Additionally, the brag book may be perceived as a crutch in the interview itself. You might find it more appropriate to utilize progressive disclosure, which is simply presenting the appropriate document at the right time during the interview. This demonstrates thought and organization and can be very positive throughout the interview. This also provides an example of your flexibility and presentation skills. Think about successes in your past that might exhibit one or more transferable skill sets. It's highly important for you to communicate how you as an individual can benefit the organization through creating revenue or other value.

Reflecting upon the past in the interview can help you describe what has brought you to this point in your career. This is why you might be having the privilege of sitting across from your interviewer right now.

Can you produce documentation regarding your past significant contributions? In other words, can you show a potential employer what you've done? It doesn't have to be elaborate. If you are just starting your career, include accomplishments in high school or college. Were you in any leadership roles? Did you have a high-grade point average or were you on the Dean's List? These are all areas to showcase on your resume.

In sales, many times documentation of rank reports, President Trophy wins, significant contest victories, and simply the ability to tie these "wins" to the prospective company's product line can help you "close the deal." No matter what area or industry you select to interview for, documentation of your accomplishments is critically important. Also, you must be able to validate your claims with supplemental awards, reports, letters, and anything else that proves your accolades. Without verifiable information, your accomplishments can simply come off as an unsubstantiated claim. This information shouldn't be given after the interview; have it with you to present with the respective accomplishment.

Randy's friend, Chad, has kept a "kudos file folder" on his laptop. This was his form of a brag book. In what probably was considered a nosey moment some years ago, Randy asked Chad what was in that file folder. His buddy indicated that it contained his accomplishments over the years. It was amazing. He had documented virtually every significant award, ranking, accolade, and praise he had received. Should he decide to interview, he could simply pull relevant pieces from the file to produce a custom "brag book." That was years ago, and Chad continues to have a great professional sales career. When he's been in a position to interview, more than likely he has had documentation of some sort to help prove his capability in that next important role. Being armed with an expansive arsenal of documentation may not be the norm, but it is extremely helpful.

If you have failed to gather performance-type information, or it simply hasn't been available to you, don't worry. Start collecting those things today. If you can obtain letters from past managers or organizations, that's great too. Look through items you may have forgotten and stored away. If you're like so many others we talk to every day, you may be surprised what you have packed away! Bring it together.

Sell yourself, but don't brag. It is great to bring a "brag book" with you to the interview that lists your accomplishments – just make sure you have the documentation to substantiate your claims.

The bottom line is that you need to consider yourself the same as a valuable product. Gather and bring all the information about what makes you who you are, and then proceed to make the very best presentation you can. One of our goals of this book is to help you learn how to best market *you*. You have quantifiable features and benefits, so you should showcase them!

Creating Your Brag Book

This feature documentation of your work is a professional portfolio of your career accomplishments. The material should be developed and utilized to substantiate the information in your resume.

When creating your brag book, have your resume in front of you to determine what information you feel is important to promote. Some examples of this would be academic awards, college transcripts and professional degrees. To validate your work ethic and past success, you may want letters of recommendation from past supervisors, coworkers, or clients. Copies of awards and sales rankings are also important to include.

We encourage you to be creative by developing your own format. For digital brag books, you will need to scan sales accomplishments, awards, photos, and other important information into one document. Use categories or dividers (i.e., education, achievements, references, photos of award ceremonies, etc.) to help you organize your brag book and make it more interesting. Never feel like you need to give out confidential information, however. Any document that is considered confidential should be treated as such. Use a black marker to cross through such information.

Scanning your documents and creating a digital copy of your information can make it easier for the interviewer to forward this information on to HR or upper-level management during the interview process. By spending the extra time creating an effective digital brag book, you will have developed an important interview tool that can be used over and over again.

While a digital copy is effective, a hard copy version of your brag book is also necessary. It is important to always bring a hard copy to the interview just in case your laptop decides not to work or the interviewer wants a copy of the material. A hard copy can be placed in a folder or three-ring binder. However you decide to present your information, make sure the folder displays professionalism. Your presentation represents you and your organizational abilities, so make it look good.

Presenting your Brag Book

If you decide to use this form of presentation during your interview, don't just read it to the interviewer. Use the material as a visual aid to reinforce an important point you are making. If you choose to present your material in an electronic format, bring your laptop to the interview. If you are uncomfortable using a brag book, practice by role playing. Know what is in your material and how to easily access specific information. For example, if the interviewer asks to see a copy of your transcript, make sure you can get to it quickly. You should be prepared by keeping a copy of your diploma and college transcript in the education section of your documentation.

For the hard copy, most individuals use a professional-looking folder or dark-colored three-ring binder for their feature documentation. In the pocket of the binder, you can place several copies of your resume to give to the interviewer. Creating sectional areas in your folder or binder will help you quickly find supportive documentation regarding your achievements. Remember, during an interview you are selling a product and that product is *you*. Everything you produce and present should show your aptitude, ability, and ambition to do a great job for the interviewer's organization.

One caveat regarding brag books is to remember to present the most relevant information in regard to the position for which you are interviewing. You may have ten different items you could present to the interviewer that have some relevance. However, there's just not time in your one-hour interview to present all of it, so pick your best. Many novice candidates will dump too much information on the interviewer. Although most managers can appreciate the volume of your accomplishments, be selective in what you present. It's important to pick out several pieces from your brag book to demonstrate relevant skill sets and performance examples of what you can do for the interviewer's company if you get the position. You can use some of the other items for future interviews if necessary.

For your first interview, prepare the top three pieces in which you can present your best example of your success and the item's transferrable relevance to the interviewer's job. This should be a great start in selling them on your past successes and how you can benefit their company. Remember, they are looking for someone who has the right experience to do the job, and if you can successfully display similar skills to what they need, you're on your way!

30-60-90 Day Plan

Although the brag book may be the most used example of presenting your past accomplishments during the interview, there are many other ways to communicate your benefits. The 30-60-90 day plan, personal websites, and even videos constitute some other examples. You can use your additional novel ideas and creativity to set yourself apart from others interviewing for the same position. I once had a candidate bring a bag filled with his sales trophies to the interview. The manager thought it showed confidence and found it unique. He got the job!

A 30-60-90 day plan is your plan for the first three months of your employment. It should include an analysis of the needs of your training, and how you intend to meet the company's objectives for performance.

To do a 30-60-90 day plan, first break the ninety-day period into three thirty-day increments. Then, consider discussing your business objectives, goals, training objectives, and any other processes or methods. If in sales, include a second page with a competitive analysis of the competitor's products and services, and an analysis of the territory to show your understanding.

There are many ways to do a 30-60-90 day plan. Be creative! Some candidates create a table-type format or a PowerPoint presentation. Either is fine if it looks professional and shows your knowledge of the company, your role, and the territory. There are many templates available online, so choose a style that you would be comfortable discussing with a hiring manager.

The following is an example of how you can present your 30-60-90 day plan.

Example 30-60-90 Day Plan:

Name: John Doe   Date: 5-18-2020

Company: XYZ Chemical Corp.   Position: Customer Service Representative

30-60-90 Day Plan

	DAY 1-30	DAY 31-60	DAY 61-90
Business Objectives/ Goals	• Meet executive staff and understand hierarchy • Gain an understanding of corporate direction relative to customers and market • Review corporate expectations regarding HR, expense management, and daily work expectations	• Review specific daily goals and expectations with manager and how to achieve these using company resources • Develop custom overall business path to success based upon current knowledge and past experience in the market • Attend meetings about company-wide sales and customer service and relay the content of the meeting to the peer team	• Review successes and areas of opportunity relative to goals over a lunch session with manager and a member of senior management • Provide presentation to senior management on how to handle customer concerns effectively • Provide a presentation to manager regarding why the company is the best overall corporate choice for their customers versus the competitors
Training Objectives	• Meet peers and direct manager • Discuss integration into the team and work assignments with peers • Establish the training calendar • Do a micro review of the company website and all product brochures to gain a deeper understanding of company offerings	• Understand customer base and begin applying objectives • Conduct field and internal work assignments with peers • Review products and services by utilizing oral quizzes and written assignments to check for understanding and future training direction	• Attend and participate in 5 customer calls weekly with current representative • Make 5 independent customer visits weekly and submit summary with outcome to manager • Develop a future plan of action (POA) for all customer calls and internal meetings

Processes/ Methods	• Review software and work completion resources • Understand use of customer relationship management (CRM) protocol • Gain an understanding of how individual performance is measured	• Review and study online customer care resources • Conduct session answering inquiries and addressing specific customer concerns with current representative oversight • Review the quality of my data entry and address any areas that need improvement	• Present a professional development workshop on best practices based upon a manager-selected topic. • Present a workshop to peers and management on best practices relative to using the CRM system. • Construct a training document on how to use company data to satisfy a customer concern

Competitor and Territory Analysis

Competitor Analysis:	Conduct a competitive analysis of two companies' products and present to management. Outline major benefits and differences between products. Identify successful sales methodologies vs. the competitors.
Territory Analysis:	Survey the assigned geography and territory. Where can an immediate impact be made? Are there areas that need immediate customer care interventions?

A word of caution: if you are copying a previously used plan or a template, make sure to proofread it well before presenting it to another employer. Presenting the wrong company name – or any other incorrect information – will definitely not help you and may keep you from moving forward.

If you have a well-written plan and you know the duties, products, and industry, bring your 30-60-90 day plan to the interview. If you don't understand the industry well, your information may not be accurate or relevant and could cause confusion for the interviewer.

Some interviewers may actually request this form of presentation for your interview. If this is requested, it's really important to have an understanding of what they want in a successful example. The best way to uncover their expectations is simply to ask for their advice regarding the expected content. Not only does this show interest and initiative on your part, it's critical to your success. Remember, the interviewer is looking at your ability to put together a coherent document so they can review your skills. This requires you to have some knowledge of their industry, which hopefully you already possess. If you don't have the luxury of that background, you'll simply have to put in the extra work and do more research.

If you are a sales representative doing a 30-60-90 day plan, start by asking them for details about their organization in the form of products, services, timelines, dollars, and other logistical items. You should be able to make a more relevant presentation based on this information. Interviewers are not usually expecting perfection, although we've seen some very good examples. The goal is to create a document where you can sell your abilities by using data and facts, not simply a product pitch. Your ability to use the supplied details of their business in a relevant fashion will hopefully put your work on top. A good presentation should provide the ammunition in getting the job done, both in landing a job and in closing a sale. So, using your researched information – along with anything else the interviewer may provide – can help you excel in putting together your customized 30-60-90 day plan.

In addition to analytics, this plan allows the employer to evaluate your organizational and/or sales abilities. Many companies utilize tools such as these to measure your knowledge. Although you may not have a total handle on their market since proprietary data usually is not available, they are interested in seeing what you create and your implementation plan. In other words, can he or she demonstrate the analysis of data and put that into a grassroots plan of action in 90 days to accomplish initial goals? This plan of action (POA) is widely used in sales, but it has been adopted by many other industries that are focused on goal-setting and accomplishment of directives within a calendar period. In many situations, developing and presenting this document in a professional manner can make or break whether you get a job offer, so take your time in constructing, reviewing, and practicing the delivery of the content.

Keep in mind that in the initial 30 days, you will be in a training mode, but by the end of a 90-day process, the company you are interviewing with will be looking for you to fully function in your position. For sales representatives, this usually equates to closed sales. How will you progress from learning about this company to actually working for them or selling their product line? Define these objectives with reasonable and measurable goals. Remember, you intend to be hired for the position, so the standards you set today may be what you are measured by tomorrow.

In summary, after the presentation of your 30-60-90 day plan, reinforce the top five reasons why you are the best choice for the position and ASK for the job!

The Personal Career Website

Many candidates have developed their own personal website to promote their resume and their credentials for interviewing purposes. This is not to be confused with a family or hobby website!

Your personal career website's sole purpose is to promote your candidacy. Obviously, it should be very professionally created, reviewed, and edited regularly. You are showcasing your talents, potentially in a variety of ways through your site. You can have documents, embedded videos, and other performance examples to help you market yourself. By having and producing this multimedia format, you're embracing technology and demonstrating your presentation skills right off the bat. When you set it up, make sure it can be presented easily and can flow between topics and documents. A menu bar along the top might be the easiest format to access these important items during an interview. Because it's designed to use in many interview scenarios, content should be very familiar and practiced.

The personal career website differs from the other previously discussed presentation types such as the 30-60-90 day plan, the brag book, or other documented achievements from your career. Where these are normally hard-copy documents to hand to the interviewer, your site is simply there to view. Typically, there will be less information than what may be found in your brag book. Because it will generally be set up for public view, its primary purpose is to entice the reader and promote your candidacy. One major benefit is that there really are no limits to the types of presentations that could be a part of this venue. Another benefit is that a candidate may link to their website on other online portals, such as a LinkedIn page. Utilizing your laptop to access and present your background and accomplishments through your website may be a great way to show your relevance and documentation. Many times, it's great for maintaining interest and interviewer engagement while selling your specific attributes. Used correctly, it could be an important tool in getting to the next step in the interview process.

Usually, this is a password-protected website and can be used on a first or subsequent interview. Is it right for all interviews? No. But, if you feel it would be good for the interviewer to see this website, then give them the link and password or show the interviewer the website during the interview.

Be prepared with hard-copy documentation of all pertinent critical documents. Due to the proximity of a laptop between the parties, sometimes projecting your information on a screen is favorable. That way you're not violating a person's personal space. Also, it generally comes off more professional using a projector and a screen. When scheduled for an interview, you can inquire into the availability and your access to their multimedia equipment onsite. Many times, the presentation part of the interview happens in the second round, so if you don't get the opportunity early, it's still okay.

Along with the hard copy resume(s), your personal career website can provide many customized presentations to review with the prospective employer and provide a "go-to" document to satisfy an interviewer's concern or simply their interest in more information. This also demonstrates your ability to master technology and move through information as needed.

As mentioned, you don't need to use this on every interview. However, your site is always there as a resource for you. Even as a review point in preparation for each interview, it has its strong points.

Now let's move on to the sixth additional way to set yourself apart from other candidates – enthusiasm!

CHAPTER SIX

Step 6 – The E in DESIRE: Enthusiasm

The last step in DESIRE is probably one of the most important steps - Enthusiasm.

Enthusiasm is a word that can bring many images immediately to your mind. For me, I picture someone who is a huge fan of a musician or band. Maybe they stood in line for hours to get into a concert or a music festival because they are dedicated and excited about seeing the artist live in concert. They wouldn't do this unless they had *enthusiasm* for the event. The concert meant something to them and because it meant something, they went out of their way to show up. It was important. Now, the same is true about a job. You may need to go out of your way to show up!

I once had a candidate drive eight hours to go to an interview. He showed up! And because of this, he got the job. Sometimes showing up is half the battle. Maybe you have been feeling overwhelmed in your job search. It's not easy. Often, going through the interview process can make you feel defeated. But my advice is to realize your worth, show up, and sell yourself! You don't have to be perfect; you just need to bring value and enthusiasm.

Enthusiasm is an important step in the process of *selling* your skills and abilities to get that job that you *want*. I emphasize those two words because you *want* to be at this juncture in the employment process – for no other reason other than you truly *want* this opportunity and you feel that you have earned it.

This brings us to the point of the "passion for the position." Whether this is evident to you or not, it will be to the interviewer. So many times, we hear about candidates getting a job offer based upon their "excitement," "energy," or "passion." Make sure you are psyched up to perform and display your enthusiasm for the position. Early on, you may not really realize how much you want the job. But becoming and staying engaged and focused during the interview process is mission critical.

Demonstrate throughout the meeting that the interviewer understands that you would "fit in" and that you would enjoy working for the organization. Again, this is the time to display your enthusiasm for going to work for their company. Let them know at the end of the interview that you want this job, and by all means, don't be afraid to tell them that.

Remember to follow-up – ask for the interviewer's business card with their contact information and then send them a thank you email as soon as possible.

Show enthusiasm and excitement about the position. Research shows that interviewers often make decisions based on who they "feel" will do the best job. Recall that decisions are not always completely based upon qualifications or past performance. People often use their gut reaction.

How to Close the Interview

We have mentioned a couple of times the importance of closing the interview. Now, let's dive a little more into how to do it.

Your passion and interest come into play when interviewing for a job. Good eye contact, a professional image, and an overall ability to communicate well will make you a strong contender for most jobs. Hopefully, all of these traits have become apparent to the interviewer and by the end of the interview process, they see you as their number one candidate for the position. But what if they are not sure? How do you find out where you stand and close the deal? The answer is to ask for their feedback and then discuss any of their concerns. After this, it is time to ask for the job.

Getting Feedback Before You Leave the Interview

Appropriate feedback from the interviewer is important to get before the interview comes to a close. Ask the interviewer, "Do you have any additional questions, concerns, or reservations about my background or my ability to perform the job?" By asking this question, you are giving permission for the interviewer to offer feedback and/or clear up any concern that may have arisen during the interview.

As recruiters, candidates are always asking for feedback after an interview. If they are not selected for the position, many want to know why. Asking this question toward the end of your interview will allow you to clear up any confusion or concern the interviewer may have and provide you with immediate feedback regarding your candidacy.

If the interviewer doesn't have any additional questions or concerns, that's great! You can move on to asking for the job.

Ask for the Job!

Don't be afraid to ask for the job! Just as a sales professional uses closing statements to sell a product, you are selling you! Asking for the next step or the position itself will only further demonstrate your enthusiasm. For instance, "Will I be included in the next step?" might be a good example of a closing statement.

You may not be a sales professional, but whatever industry or position you are interviewing for, asking for the job is a must. It shows you *want* the position. If you don't ask for the next step in the interview process, the manager may assume you were not that interested in the position. If you can look the interviewer in the eye and tell them that you will work hard for them (and mean it), you will gain their respect and may even get the job.

Make sure during the meeting that the interviewer knows throughout the process that you are extremely interested in the position and that you want this job. Stay engaged mentally and physically and maintain your energy throughout the process. Sometimes, employers have multiple meetings or interviews with the candidate to ensure the consistency of their interview performance. The interviewers may be simply checking to see that the candidate maintains energy and interest throughout the entire interview process.

Think through your responses so that they display confidence versus arrogance. Closing for the next step in the process might also include statements like, "When will you be making your decision regarding this position or what is the next step in the process?" When you ask an interviewer this question, it shows them your level of interest – plus you are finding out important information about the timeline of your own job search.

Additionally, don't forget to show confidence in the process. A statement such as, "From what we've discussed today, would you extend me an offer or move me forward in the process?" helps to show interest and confidence. You may be premature in asking for the offer if the previous discussion indicates that there will be additional interviews. However, it is important to demonstrate this high level of interest in the position and show your sincere desire to move forward in the process.

This is probably the most important tip we offer! Whatever the type of interview and whatever phase you are in regarding the hiring process, continue to close with each person you interview with by asking them for the job! Your enthusiasm and passion for the position will set you apart from other candidates, and you will show the interviewer you have confidence in your abilities. You may say, "I don't feel comfortable selling to get a job."

Well, neither do most other candidates! If you're a "little over the top," no problem. They're probably looking for engaged and energetic additions to their team.

As a branch of this, you should also be making interviewing a priority. If an HR representative or a recruiter contacts you to schedule an interview on a certain time and day, you should make all efforts to accommodate their schedule. It should not be the other way around. Telling a scheduler that you need to coach a little league game and can't go at that time may end your chances of interviewing for the position. If the little league game is important to you, then it may be worth it, but if you can make the interview, you might get the job. It is all about setting priorities. Being courteous and respectful and prioritizing an interviewer's time is crucial. It will set you apart from other candidates.

Let's get back to the basics. Obviously, most companies realize that experience is important. They use this background so that they may assess a person's successes in the sales environment. But experience isn't everything.

We know attitude is just as important. It is very difficult, if not impossible, to coach or teach enthusiasm. The passion and energy of an employee is critical and potentially contagious to the rest of the team. If employees are not excited about their goods and services, then how is the customer supposed to get that way?

As a final thought, you've heard the adage, "Control what you can control." Well, as a candidate, an individual can control their excitement toward a sought-after position. Likewise, an employer should exhibit a similar excitement level regarding the presentation of their company, including their goods and services. For an appropriate hire to occur, both parties should be "sold" on each other and be truly excited about future opportunities.

Thank-You Notes

There are many ways to show an employer your desire to work for them. We have discussed a few of these, but communication is the most important. Through follow-up communication and thank-you notes, you can show your continued enthusiasm. Let's discuss how and when you should communicate.

It's amazing how thank-you notes have become a thing of the past. Think about how often you may have given someone a gift – maybe for a graduation or birthday present? Now reflect upon how often you have received a thank-you note from that person. In today's fast-paced world, we often forget the niceties. We may not intentionally mean to forget to send thank-you notes, but let's face it – this is just something not very many people prioritize these days. However, after an interview, a thank-you note is a must.

Emailing a thank-you note is great! Hiring managers are looking for employees with good follow-up skills. Immediately after your interview, email all parties involved in the interview a thank-you note. This is crucial! As a reminder, collect the business cards from your interviewers. Their cards will usually contain their email addresses to use to follow up with them.

A well-written thank-you note sent by email to the interviewer(s) will make you stand out. It is another way to get your name in front of the decision-maker and another chance to close or sell the employer on you. Do it immediately, at least within four hours, if possible. By responding quickly, you show that you are organized and interested. The employer will make the assumption that you will also respond to their customers in the same fashion.

In addition, you may want to also send a handwritten thank-you note in the mail. This will put your name in front of the interviewer one more time. You might think this may sound over the top. Maybe so, but enthusiasm goes a long way in getting a job.

Not sending a thank-you note can be a deal breaker for some managers. In the mind of many, it is an absolute necessity to move forward in the process. It can show a sincere interest in the interviewer's time, excitement regarding the opportunity, and interest in moving forward. In fact, if it's not done, it can certainly be noticeably absent in comparison to the other candidates for the position. For the investment in your time, a thank-you note is golden. The following is an example of a thank you note to show your enthusiasm to an employer.

Example Thank-You Note:

Street Address
City, State, Zip Code

Date

Hiring Manager Name
Title
Street Address
City, State , Zip Code

Re: Job Title

Dear Hiring Manager: (include a personal title such as Ms., Mrs., Mr., or Dr, if possible)

Thank you for taking time to meet with me today concerning the _____ (job title) position with _____ (company name). After discussing the position with you further, I am even more convinced that I would succeed in the role and challenges of this position.

I appreciate the time you spent discussing _____(give specific example of something discussed during interview). My strengths in building strong customer relationships and knowledge of the sales process will allow me to exceed my sales goals and close business for _____ (company name). I have a strong work ethic. Please be assured that if given the opportunity, I will work hard for you and _____. (company name)

_____ (Company Name) has an outstanding reputation, and I am honored and excited to have the opportunity to possibly join this organization and your team.

If I can provide you with additional information regarding my past accomplishments, education or qualifications, please contact me at the phone number listed below.

Sincerely,

Your Signature

Your Name

Your Phone Number

No Longer Interested in the Position

As professionals, we know that not every interaction with an employer works out. Maybe you have met with an interviewer and feel that you just wouldn't fit into their organization or team. Whatever the reason, there just wasn't a spark, and you are ready to move on. So, where do you go from here? How do you let the person or company know you are not interested?

The truth is, it isn't always easy, but it is necessary. If you were dating someone and then didn't want to see them again, shouldn't you let them know? Often, people just try to fade away from the relationship, a term referred to today as "ghosting." But this lack of response actually portrays a lack of respect for the individual. The Merriam-Webster dictionary defines ghosting as "the act or practice of abruptly cutting off all contact with someone (such as a former romantic partner) by no longer accepting or responding to phone calls, instant messages, etc."[5]

According to Liz Lewis, in an article for Indeed;

> "Job seekers ghost at different stages in the hiring process: 50% have skipped on a scheduled job interview, and 46% say they stopped responding to calls and emails from potential employers. Others ditch when they're farther along: 19% have accepted a verbal offer and disappeared before signing the paperwork, and 22% have not shown up for their first day of work at least once.
>
> In turn, employers are getting ghosted at every stage of the hiring process, leaving them scrambling to respond. The vast majority (84%) have had candidates not show up for interviews, and 64% say they stopped communicating with no explanation. Nearly 60% report candidates accepting a verbal offer only to disappear. And a stunning 65% of employers report no-shows on their first day of work."[6]

You have probably heard of "ghosting" many times but have not thought about its impacts. The sad fact is that employers will remember how they were treated during the interview process, and this will impact your reputation. Remember to treat employers with respect. To let them know you are no longer interested in the position, send the interviewer or human resource representative a short email. You don't have to create an elaborate excuse, just simply tell them that you have decided to pursue another opportunity. This allows the employer to move forward with other candidates and protects your professional reputation. It is important not to

[5] Merriam Webster, Accessed July 8, 2019 through https://www.merriam-webster.com/dictionary/ghosting
[6] Indeed 2019. Lewis, Liz *The Ghosting Guide: An Inside Look at Why Job Seekers Disappear.* August 26. Accessed May 9, 2020 http://blog.indeed.com/2019/08/26/ghosting-guide/

burn bridges and keep your professional relationships strong.

And there you have it! The six steps of DESIRE. Each of these steps will help you to win the job of your dreams. Now, we are going to assume you had some great interviews, the company has selected you, and you will be receiving a job offer. Let's discuss more about what to look for in a job offer and how to negotiate your salary.

◖ CHAPTER SEVEN

Income

Ah, the question of money! The reason you need to work, right? Although important to you, your salary expectations or requirements are not as important to the interviewer. They want to know what skills and abilities you bring to the company first before they are willing to give you an offer. Because of this, it is important to let the interviewer bring up the subject of money first. You may be in your third interview, and the topic has still not been discussed. This can happen. This is when being prepared will be most valuable to you. If you know what you are worth, when the time comes, you can address the topic with more confidence.

Salary Expectations/Requirements

One way to know your worth is to do some online research. There are multiple websites that allow you to search a job title in a particular city and state to give you a point of reference. You might ultimately need to decide if you would take a position for less, but it can still be a good guide.

If you were lucky enough to be asked during the interview process about your salary expectations, answer this question as upfront as possible. A good answer might be that you are currently making "x" dollars and you would like to get a 10 percent increase in order to feel that you are moving your career forward. Think about how you want to answer this question before you start interviewing. If you don't want to disclose your current salary, consider asking the interviewer what the compensation is for the role and then letting them know if that amount is acceptable.

The laws are changing. At the time this book was written, there are several local and state governments within the United States that have banned an employer from asking questions about salary history. According to the article, "Salary history bans: A running list of states and localities that have outlawed pay history questions":

> "State and local governments are increasingly adopting laws and regulations that prohibit employers from requesting salary history information from job applicants.
>
> The laws are aimed at ending the cycle of pay discrimination and some go further than merely banning pay history questions. A few also prohibit an employer from relying on an applicant's pay history to set compensation if discovered or volunteered; others prohibit an employer from taking disciplinary action against employees who discuss pay with coworkers."[7]

To view a running list of state and localities banning salary history, visit

---

[7] HR Dive, 2-18-20 *Salary history bans: A running list of states and localities that have outlawed pay history questions.* https://www.hrdive.com/news/salary-history-ban-states-list/516662/ Accessed 3/19/20.

https://www.hrdive.com/news/salary-history-ban-states-list/516662/.

No matter how the employer asks the question, it is up to you to know how to answer it. If you do not want to disclose your current salary, then don't. It is perfectly fine to say that you would like to negotiate your salary based upon your experience and what you have to offer the company.

Job Offers

You have worked hard getting to this point. The company wants to hire you and now is offering you the position. Let's discuss the key areas for you to consider.

First, ask for the offer in writing. While verbal offers are often given first, don't be afraid to ask for a written job offer. At a minimum, the written offer should include:

- The title of the position
- Salary
- Start date
- Commissions, bonus plans if applicable
- Benefits (health, dental, vision, 401K, paid time off, etc.)
- Be alert to contingencies (successful background check, drug screening, etc.)

Most companies will allow you to review their benefit package prior to employment. This is a great time to ask questions. It is also a great time to bring up any dates that you will need time off. For example, if you have a wedding planned and will need particular dates off, tell the employer up front. Don't wait until after you start employment. Employers don't like surprises. Since you most likely will not have any paid-time-off accumulated, be courteous and let them know ahead of time so they can plan. This is important since most companies have a training plan in place for new employees, and they will need to schedule you accordingly. Most employers will try to accommodate reasonable requests, especially if they know about it prior to your job acceptance.

If you are given an offer that is not as high as you would like, talk with the employer regarding your salary needs. Provide them sound reasoning behind your request. Keep in mind though, once you make your counter-offer to them for additional money or benefits, their original offer may no longer be available to you. Again, if you decide to ask for a higher salary, be sure the employer understands why. You might start the discussion by first letting the employer know that you do *want* the position. Then, tell the employer you would accept the position at $___ amount. Make sure you give the employer a definite number that you are willing to accept. The last thing an employer wants to do is get an approval for an increase in the offer, and then it is still not acceptable.

If you are given an offer that is acceptable, don't delay! You should not have to think about it for days. If you do, it is probably not the opportunity for you. You want to show your new employer you *want* the job, and you're excited about embarking on your new career. You can do this by accepting the offer within 24 hours. Delays in the process will make it look as though you have other offers or that you are just not that excited about the opportunity.

There are many other considerations when deciding to accept an offer from an employer. Here are some other benefits that might also weigh into your decision:

- Sign-on bonuses, commission
- Vacation, paid time-off
- Tuition reimbursement
- Health, dental, vision
- Retirement, 401K plans, profit sharing, stock options
- Leadership training programs
- Work-life balance
- Advancement in title – maybe you are looking for a promotion, and it is more important to you than a specific monetary amount. I recently had an employer change the title of a position to encompass the candidate's career goals. Sometimes, it is the little things that matter most.

It is important to consider the whole offer. You may be offered less in salary, but the company's tuition reimbursement plan or healthcare plan may benefit you more in the long run, and therefore, outweigh the difference. One way to compare your current or past position with the current opportunity is to create a "pros and cons" list and to think about "net" numbers. It can be as simple as pulling out a piece of paper and creating two columns, maybe one labeled "Current Employer" and the other labeled "Prospective Employer." Then, you can be more objective in the assessment. Create line-items such as salary, bonus, health insurance, 401K, company car, vacation, retirement, tuition reimbursement, and the like. Identify those areas that are different between the two organizations and place a monetary value to each one.

For instance, if your future opportunity includes a car and your existing role does not, maybe that's a $10K annual benefit favoring the new opportunity. Ultimately, when totaling your columns, there will be a $10K increase in your "net" column for the new role. Conversely, if the current position has much better healthcare coverage in the annual amount of $5K, then this amount would be favorable in the current column. This is simplistic, but it works. The total in each column can help you make more of an objective decision.

	Current Employer	Prospective Employer
Salary	$50,000	$55,000
Bonus	$3,000	$6,000
Healthcare	$10,000	$5,000
401K	equal	equal
Other Benefits	No tuition reimbursement	Tuition reimbursement - $5,000
Company Car	None	$10,000
TOTAL:	$63,000	$81,000

(may include paid-time off, sick leave, tuition reimbursement, dental & vision insurance, etc.)

The evaluation chart is just one example of how to create a tool for decision making. There are many ways that you can assess an opportunity. However,

I would encourage you to remove as much emotion as possible and create a more data driven, objective view of your upcoming career decision.

After inputting the variables and arriving at the totals, it makes it easier to make an objective decision between your current and potential future employment. Taking out any other subjective considerations, the prospective opportunity appears to be a good choice. Of course, the subjective considerations such as stability of the organization, demand for the product or service and your overall perceived quality of the opportunity organization are important, too.

Earlier, we discussed that interviewers will sometimes make instinctual, gut reactions relative to making a hiring decision. As a candidate, you may find yourself doing the same. When the facts are all reviewed, there's still a final decision to be made as to whether the decision is the correct move for you. We're all human and this humanistic, sometimes emotional part of potential change can be hard. If you feel like you'll fit in and be an integral part of your next opportunity along with achieving better compensation, then you're probably on the right track. It can be a challenge, even if you have your ducks in a row. As my father has said for years, "Sometimes, there are no easy answers."

Don't overlook a couple of final considerations when evaluating an opportunity; it's very important to consider work-life balance. The impact of a balanced life between work and a personal/family life cannot be overestimated. Even though you may not be able to give it a monetary value, work-life balance should still weigh into your overall decision.

Does the potential opportunity require extensive travel? Will you work weekends? The logistics and requirements of the role need to generally line up for your overall happiness and satisfaction to occur. It's important for both you and your new employer for this arrangement to be a match. There is also a close correlation between job satisfaction and success in a position, so review the job description once again and question any areas of potential uncertainty.

If you have just graduated from high school or college, or you're in the unfortunate situation of losing your employment, what steps should you take? How do you plan or replan your future career? We will discuss this in the next two chapters.

⟨🔥⟩ CHAPTER EIGHT

Career Planning… and Replanning

The majority of people plan a career starting with their choice of education and what skills seem to be a natural fit for them. While this tactic works for some people, it doesn't always work for everyone. Creating a career plan is important. However, many candidates seem to fall into their next career rather than planning for it. Let's change that trajectory.

It may have been some time since you thought about your professional objective. Candidates often write up some type of objective statement to put on their resume, but what does it really mean to them? It's not easy to think about all the facets of modern life. A career is certainly important, but it should reflect what you want out of your life in its entirety. Planning your career early on may save you from a potential misstep in the future. Change can and will happen, but having a general roadmap of where you want to be at certain milestones will help you achieve both your professional and personal goals.

Let's get started. Before you develop a career plan, do some thinking about your career and what you want to achieve with your next career move. If you have just begun your career, this may not be as easy. However, if you have more than five years of experience, consider what you have enjoyed most during these years? Think about what companies you have worked for and if the company's culture fit your style. If it didn't, what type of industry would you enjoy? Experience is a great teacher in determining your future happiness in a role. When you like what you do, it's generally evident to all, including yourself.

You may have heard the old saying, "Find something you love to do and you will never work a day in your life." I have heard it often, and typically it is recited by people who seem to have found their calling. Examples of this might be people who love to read and become writers or book editors, or maybe individuals who love playing music or sports. Sometimes they are even able to become professionals and turn their passions into money. But what if you are not able to move your hobby into a profession? There has to be an alternate plan. It's good to have that safety-net handy.

How do you know if you *want* a position? We all know that it is important to be practical with our dreams. If you are a great baker, then it makes sense that you could open a bakery and make a living. However, if you love water-skiing, like Randy does, it doesn't mean he should become a professional water-skier. Taking time to study the market before starting a new business venture is important. The same is true about career planning.

If you created a career plan early in life based upon your interests and aptitude, your dream job may not be in question. If you are studying to be a lawyer, doctor, or other professional, you are investing many years into your career plan to achieve big rewards. However, there may be occasions where even if you have created a solid career plan, you may have to still replan due to unplanned detours that can happen in each of our lives (i.e., lay-offs, health issues, marriage, divorce, etc.). Detours are not always led by our desires; sometimes they are out of necessity.

These career detours are sometimes a blessing. We are in a free society, so we have the liberty to change directions. Personally, I have enjoyed two different careers. I started my career as a registered nurse working in the field of oncology, caring for cancer patients. I gave chemotherapy, assisted with procedures, and cared for people as they underwent treatments. I felt I was doing important work that gave meaning to my life. After working at the hospital for several years, I transitioned into hospice nursing to care for patients in their homes. Taking time with patients and improving the quality of their lives was important to me, and I loved what I did.

The opportunity to move into a mid-management role (managing a team of hospice nurses) became available. I struggled with the thought of no longer being a field nurse. Would I be happy not being actively involved in patient care? After all, I loved nursing and working with cancer patients, but I decided to give it a try. By stepping outside of my comfort zone, I found out that I did have other skills that I enjoyed just as much as nursing. I loved teaching and mentoring others.

Perhaps you, too, have other skills you have not reflected upon yet. Stepping out of your comfort zone is important relative to career development. I had a manager say to me once, "Generally, people are either getting better or worse." At the time, I thought this was a rather crass statement, but it's true. As professionals, we should be bettering ourselves every day. Whether that is reading within our trade, taking additional classes, or simply being mentored by others; we need to be better than we were yesterday.

Reflecting back, leading my team of hospice nurses challenged me in ways that I had not been challenged in the past. I learned new leadership skills, like how to manage processes and people. These newfound and developed skills opened doors for me to other management roles in healthcare. You will be surprised at what you can do, too! No one is perfect; you will trip and sometimes fall in your endeavors. I've done it many times. But you must learn from your experiences, get up, and move on.

In 1997, Randy and I were blessed to have a daughter. After having her in daycare, she kept getting ill with RSV (a respiratory virus mostly affecting children). Due to recurrent infections, the pediatrician advised me to take her out of daycare for a while. At that time, Randy and I made the decision that it would be best for me to stay home with her.

As a new stay-at-home mother, I worked on-call for hospice, but I knew I wanted to do something other than hospital and home health nursing. I just wasn't sure what else I could do with my nursing background. Since I had gained management skills, I thought about what I enjoyed most about being a manager. I loved building teams.

While home with my daughter, I would receive phone calls from recruiters interested in recruiting Randy. He was in sales. I would talk with the recruiters and referred several people to them. I would listen to the description of the job and refer people I knew. After matching several people to these job opportunities, I wondered about working as a recruiter myself. That's how our company, Global Edge Recruiting, began.

In fact, I took my first job order from a large medical device company while my daughter was very noisy in the background. Trying to get away from her "excitement" and knowing that she was fine (and just a little cranky), I headed to the back of the house with only a pen in my hand. I listened intently to the hiring manager tell me what he was looking for in a potential employee. Wow, I was unprepared for my new role as a recruiter! I didn't have anything to write on – not a piece of paper in sight! I had to quickly think. What could I use? As a last resort, I jotted the information for the job on a piece of toilet paper. It worked.

There have been many days where I wish I would have kept that piece of toilet paper. Most businesses keep their first dollar bill... not me! A scribbled-on piece of toilet paper marked the start of my business. Now, that's not only humbling, but kind of humorous, isn't it?

The point is that just because your education lies in one area, it doesn't mean you are stuck with that vocation for the rest of your life. You can do something else with it. If you notice, I have a BSN (Bachelors of Science in Nursing), but after several years of recruiting, I felt I needed more education in my field and later returned to school to obtain a Master's degree in Human Resource Development and an additional certification in my field, called a

Senior Professional in Human Resources (SPHR) awarded from the Human Resource Certification Institute.

Randy has also enjoyed several occupations. He began his education by getting a Bachelor's degree in marketing and management while working in retail and starting a career in real estate sales. As a young salesperson, he became a managing broker of a real estate office and later taught courses at a pre-licensure school for those wanting to enter the field. After a few years of teaching, he decided to go back to school and receive an additional educational degree to be able to teach secondary level (high school) business and science. During this time, he was approached for a position in outside sales with Xerox. It was a great opportunity, and it was early in our marriage. He put the teaching degree aside and decided to take this position to gain business-to-business sales experience. It was his business-to-business sales success that then led him to pharmaceutical and medical sales.

Fast forward twenty years, after enjoying a career in the medical sales industry, Randy decided to transition to the recruiting business and joined me in recruiting medical and pharmaceutical salespeople at Global Edge.

Life is full of detours, and often those detours involve our careers. For example, maybe your company is asking you to relocate or asking you to assume a different role. Times of change can be scary. You may be at a crossroads in your life. You may want to make a career move, or maybe not so much. Through displacement or termination, you may have been placed in a position in which you are forced to make a change. We have all been there, whether through our own choice or the choice of someone else. We are forced into making a change, and change can be scary. It is times like these when developing a new plan may be in order.

When this occurs, take the time to pause and look at your career. Career reflection can help you pursue your dreams personally and professionally. You may have heard the old adage about the "past is the past" or "everything is smaller in the rear-view mirror." Yes, the past is truly the past and you can't change your history, but you can use the past to strengthen your career future. What successes have you had? Ask yourself, where do you see yourself in five years? By analyzing where you have been and taking time to evaluate where you are going, you can create a strategic plan for your career. Why sit back and let fate determine where you work and what your next job will be? Wouldn't it be more satisfying to develop a career plan and work hard to make it happen?

We hear about work-life balance often, and it's more than just a cliché. It's important. When you've found the role that you truly desire, you're happier, more satisfied, and more engaged in work and life. Work-life balance is easier to achieve when you've found the right job.

Downsized? Now What?

The economy is always changing. Technological advances, new products, and advances in research and development can cause disruption or a shift in the market.

There are two types of hiring markets. One is an employer's market and the other is called a candidate's market. As the economy changes, the pendulum swings back and forth from one to the other. In the early 2000s, as well as in 2020 during the COVID-19 pandemic, without question, it is an employer's market. There are very few jobs available, and there are numerous candidates available. This allows employers the ability to interview and hire easily with less competition. In an employer's market, talent is plentiful. Because there may be an abundance of candidates to fill limited positions, some organizations may take advantage of this scenario in their attitudes and direction.

However, things are different in a candidate's market. When the pendulum swings to a candidate-driven market, the candidates' talents are now in demand, and many times candidates are able to choose from multiple opportunities. This sets a different tone in the job market; employers are no longer in the driver's seat. This can be unfortunate for some prospective employers who do not realize the change has occurred. If they are not as cordial or flexible in their dealings with potential candidates, they will lose a large portion of the available candidate pool during this period.

In a booming economy, it is much more difficult to find high-quality prospects in some industries because candidates have their choice of job opportunities. In a candidate's market, time is of the essence. Hiring managers need to be aware of how long their hiring process takes and move candidates quickly through each stage so the company does not lose the best candidates to competitors.

If you have been working for the past few years, you may have seen both the employer's market and the candidate's market. In the recent employer's market, you may have either been downsized, experienced the fear of possible downsizing, or have seen one of your colleagues downsized. Unfortunately, there are many industries that seem to be restructuring, realigning, or right-sizing their employees.

If you are one of the many people currently experiencing downsizing, don't let it stop you from moving on and possibly moving up with your next career move. The past negative stereotype of a downsized employee is no longer true. Some of the best people get downsized due to company mergers, acquisitions, and occasionally just due to poor corporate planning. Companies are hopeful and forecast large sales numbers and then fail to meet their predictions. Sometimes employee restructuring may be due to manufacturing issues, lack of product approvals, label changes, or competitive entries into the marketplace. Competitive products sometimes establish a more favorable market position. A company can simply take the lead within a market segment through superior marketing or the perception or reality of superior data. This can lead to a competitive company needing to cut costs, and thereafter, personnel. However it happens, there is not much that can be done about the volatility in different markets because most industries remain dynamic and are always changing to meet the demands of their customers.

Greg Heslin, on the website *All About Business*, does a great job at defining these terms. He writes:

> "Downsizing is the act of reducing the number of employees on a company's payroll and is considered different than layoffs. Downsizing is scaling down the number of employees permanently rather than temporarily like layoffs. Employees who are laid off usually have a good chance at being rehired, whereas those who are victims of downsizing do not."[8]

So, back to the original question: You've been downsized... now what? President Harry S. Truman once said, "It's a recession when your neighbor loses his job; it's a depression when you lose yours."[9] The most important point to realize is that even if you were let go from a particular company, you are still valuable. Downsizing can be hard – on even the most confident person's ego – and without confidence, it is hard to sell yourself during the interview process.

If you have not been downsized yet but it remains a possibility with your current employer, start a file now to use for your "brag book." As we have discussed previously, gather your achievements now, and if you are later downsized, remember to get a letter of reference from the employer indicating you were not dismissed based upon performance. These steps will help remove all doubt from any potential employers' minds about why you are not currently employed.

[8] Heslin, Greg 2007, Layoffs and Downsizings in 2007, All About Business
http://business-view-9-co.50webs.com/layoffs-and-downsizing-in-2007-261956.html Accessed 2-28-20
[9] Forbes Quotes, Thoughts on the Business of Life,
https://www.forbes.com/quotes/10624/ Accessed 2-28-20

It is also important to note the number of employees the company has recently downsized. Document the number of downsizing waves you were able to make it through prior to being dismissed. Why? Because if you were the one person a company chose to dismiss out of 300 employees, this statistic is harder to overcome than if the company dismissed 50 percent of their workforce. Hiring managers are often analytical people and will look at numbers. Statistics relative to realignments are a great way to communicate what occurred with your last employer and why.

The Severance Package

If you were lucky enough to be given a severance package, it is important to use this time wisely.

- **Start interviewing as soon as possible.** When interviewing, keep an open mind about opportunities and evaluate each company and their pipeline (potential future products) to avoid being laid-off in the future. Keep in mind, however, the longer you wait to get another position, the more difficult it will be to get hired.
- **Try to select job opportunities that match your skill sets.** For example, if you sold a cardiovascular drug, think about applying for a medical device sales position selling to cardiologists. If you have established relationships or skills in a particular area, that experience is valuable to potential employers.

You have been and are still valuable, so relax and trust in yourself and your abilities! Read articles and books to keep yourself current on your industry's news. Review your own personal direction and career needs and with all of this information, refocus your career goals. Take some time to revise your resume and to reinvent yourself. Talk to your past associates and friends to find out which products and companies are "up and coming." It's an overused cliché, but now is the time to network. Employment leads and opportunities can arrive in non-traditional ways – use your imagination. Be optimistic and utilize your resources. Remember, many individuals have found opportunities because they have been forced into change. They moved on to successful, even more rewarding positions. You can too!

Years ago, when Randy was downsized from a company, we found this quote helpful:

> *"God, grant me the serenity to accept the things I cannot change; courage to change the things I can, and wisdom to know the difference."*
> ~ Reinhold Niebuhr

No matter what your belief system, it is important to note that there are things in life that can be changed and then other things that might be more difficult to change. By working on your personal brand (cover letters, resumes, etc.,) you are choosing to focus on important areas in your life where you can have an impact. Sometimes it is hard to see that when you are in the midst of a storm.

Eventually, after a few months, Randy was able to find a position that was superior to his last role. It wasn't easy. He interviewed with several companies before he landed a position. While he wasn't necessarily patient, he was persistent.

As you encounter circumstances that you do not have the ability to change, remember it takes courage and wisdom to move forward. If you are in this situation, realize you are not alone. Reach out to friends and past coworkers to start networking and don't give up. A better opportunity is waiting for you!

Here are a few areas to consider when career planning or replanning after being downsized:

Education

If you are trying to get your first job or you've been realigned, maybe it's time to take a look at your educational background. Taking a few extra classes to finish that master's degree might just give you the slight edge over your competition. Education is an objective area an employer can review. Many times, when all the variables are equal, an advanced education can help. It's not just the degree; it's the recognized effort that you put forward to receive these credentials.

Target your Applications

Use job search tools like Indeed.com to find jobs in your area. Read the job requirements and ask yourself what skills you have that would be similar to the requirements set by the employer in their advertisement. If you don't have any of the requirements set forth by the employer, then you most likely will not get selected. If you have some of the requirements, then sell your background and skills in a cover letter to the employer.

Job Continuity

One thing to consider when replanning your career is how often you change jobs. Recently, we had a candidate that had four different jobs within a four-year period. While these types of situations (lay-offs, reductions in force, downsizings) can happen to anyone, it is highly unlikely that it would occur four times within such a short period.

Typically, the industry standard (at least in sales) is no more than three jobs in a ten-year period. Of course, if someone has been downsized, employers will take this into consideration. A potential employer may want to know how many other people were laid off. They may ask for references to substantiate your claim. Think ahead and include this information in a cover letter or on your resume. If you have any gaps in your work history, be ready to explain this to potential employers or simply address it on your resume.

Lastly, don't give up. Everyone has to start somewhere. Take time to figure out what unique qualities you have to offer when applying for a position. Then, after you have thoroughly researched the role, plan your strategy and go out and sell your credentials and abilities to that prospective employer.

The quest for a new job is easier when you have contacts. But networking doesn't have to be just with people you know. You can also reach out to people you don't know. Most people are willing to help others during difficult times.

Don't forget the importance of networking. Let's discuss how networking can help you.

⟨🔥⟩ CHAPTER NINE

The Importance of Networking

For our purposes, the definition of networking is the exchange of information or services among individuals, groups, or institutions.[10] Networking actually is a very basic form of communication. Just like you visit with friends and family on a personal level, a more professional meeting can be with business individuals or others with beneficial connections into areas of your interest.

As you're probably aware, this can be very important to a career and overall

---

[10] *Merriam-Webster Dictionary*. (2020, May 9th). Retrieved from https://www.merriam-webster.com/dictionary/networking

success. It's important to be open to networking. Believe it or not, most people still want to help others. You're not going to be disliked for seeking information to further your career, in fact quite the opposite. Many employers and other key decision-makers appreciate the tenacity of those that inquire, ask questions, and are excited about someone or their business.

I know we've mentioned this a lot, but enthusiasm is important and contagious. Still, some may feel they are averse to attempting to network with others. But by simply putting yourself out there, you will find that it's not that hard and many times quite enjoyable. Connecting with others can help you open doors that may not be available to you with just a resume and a list of accomplishments. Think of networking as the master key to unlock opportunities.

Typically, you may be surfing the internet, reviewing job boards, hitting social networking sites, and submitting resumes online for consideration. The problem with that singular approach is that many times you'll end up in a digital pile. Harsh, but true. Obviously, it's important to do those things; just don't make it your only approach. There is no question that surfing the internet has been successful in finding employment over the last couple of decades. But there is more to finding the job you really want! Don't underestimate the power of face-to-face career networking in addition to your other job search activities. By meeting and connecting with other professionals and letting them know your goals, you will become more exposed to potential opportunities. In fact, your connections can potentially bring your resume up from the bottom of that digital pile to a real-life memorable candidate that the employer will interview.

Still, social networking is a very important part of your overall networking strategy. These sites have changed the way humans communicate in the 21st century. Websites such as LinkedIn, Facebook, Twitter, and Instagram have proven that people all across the globe are connected in one way or another.

If you have not efficiently tapped into the social networking sites during your job search, you may need to consider utilizing this important tool. On sites such as these, you showcase your resume and accomplishments by posting your profile for free.

Your LinkedIn Profile

Groups are an important tool on LinkedIn and Facebook. On LinkedIn, being a member of a particular group will permit you to easily contact members. The more groups you are involved in, the better your network of potential employers will become. Becoming a fan or a group member of various company Facebook pages can open doors to potential opportunities. Additionally, employers and recruiters post new job opportunities for their fans to follow.

Create a professional look on your profile. Use a high-quality headshot with a simple background for your picture. Dress professionally in your photo. Create a cover photo that is also professional or just use the standard templates provided.

There are a few other ways you can update your LinkedIn profile to get noticed by hiring managers and recruiters. The area below your name on LinkedIn (the headline) is often noticed first when someone visits your page. At the time of our publication, this area allows for 120 characters. It is also very important for someone finding you through keywords. For instance, I am a recruiter that specializes in medical device and pharmaceutical sales. Because of this, the area below my name says, "CEO & Founder – Global Edge Recruiting | Medical Device Sales Recruiter | Career Consultant | Author of "HIRE with FIRE". I specifically used the term, "Medical Device Sales Recruiter," because that is a keyword that someone searching LinkedIn might use to find a medical device sales recruiter. You might need to be creative with this area. Remember, however, that employers can see this information, so if you are currently employed be careful with what you write. If you are not employed, adding a phrase such as, "Seeking a position in…" might help the reader know you are interested in employment.

The summary or "about" area typically allows for 100+ words. Optimize this area by using important keywords. Make it about what you can offer a company. What skills do you have that would help a company grow?

Be sure to put your jobs and list accomplishments on your profile. Human resource managers, hiring managers, and recruiters are always looking for talent. By optimizing your LinkedIn profile, adding keywords, previous employment, and accomplishments, employers will find you. If you need help finding keywords, use the search bar to look at of the most commonly used search terms. Also, ask for recommendations from coworkers, past supervisors, and friends. This adds credibility.

Lastly, consider if you want to make your LinkedIn profile public or private. If you have spent time developing and optimizing your LinkedIn profile, add it to the top of your resume. If you have not, leave it off.

Other Ways to Network

As we mentioned earlier in this chapter, don't just leave your career networking to online networking sites. Many communities and industries have associations that meet on a regular monthly basis. For instance, if you are in medical or pharmaceutical sales, many cities will have a local representative association. There are thousands of these types of groups within various disciplines in industry, government, HR, and education. For example, I am a member of the Society of Human Resource Professionals, and we have a local organization that meets monthly. The networking potential is great! Attend one of these meetings and hand out your resume since promoting your candidacy is key. Your friends may be able help as well. Give them a copy of your resume and ask them to give it to their manager. Most people are happy to help when they realize your sincere interest.

Don't be afraid to put yourself out there. Initiate contact at all levels. Talk to your friends that work in the area in which you are interested, join social networking sites like LinkedIn, and cold-call on companies to see if they have openings. Effectively, your new job is to find one! Work to find those openings and then do whatever is necessary to make the interview at the prospect's convenience. Yes, you may have to drive 100 miles, but be excited about the opportunity and show it.

Working with Recruiters

To work with a recruiter, you must first understand how recruiters are paid. Recruiters, also called headhunters, have contracts with many companies to assist in locating and recruiting the best talent for that company. When a candidate is placed in a position, the recruiter is paid a placement fee for their work. Although mindful of employment law, EEOC guidelines, and ethics, a recruiting firm or executive search firm's first allegiance is to their client, the company, not the candidate.

An employment agency, on the other hand, works for candidates. Candidates can be charged a fee or a percentage of their earnings to find them a position. For this reason, it is important to understand the difference.

While most recruiters are willing to provide guidance during the interview process for their candidates, their ultimate goal is to get the best person hired for the position so that their client is satisfied. This is why it is important to sell yourself and your abilities to recruiters. If you have great achievements, let them know what those achievements are and how they relate to the position. Recruiters love having those important nuggets of information to sell to their clients.

If you are not interested in an opportunity, let the recruiter know. Be upfront. Keep track of which job opportunities are presented to you by a specific recruiter. Many companies utilize multiple recruiting firms, even sometimes representing the same open position. Similar to the field of real estate, recruiters earn their compensation through completion of the task. They are compensated once a candidate is placed within a role. Be mindful of which recruiter is working on a particular opening for you. Nothing upsets the process more than two recruiters presenting the same candidate for the same position. Candidates often think this helps their case, but companies may become perturbed when the process becomes confusing.

Stay in touch with your recruiter during the interview process. Recruiters often know the hiring manager and what qualities they find desirable relative to candidates. If you don't communicate effectively with your recruiters, you are losing out on valuable information that could put you ahead of other candidates.

Send your recruiter a thank-you note for their assistance, even if you do not get the job. This will keep you in the loop for future positions. Hiring managers develop relationships with recruiters and often trust their judgment.

♦ CONCLUSION

"Dream big!"

If I close my eyes, I can still hear my mother encouraging me to dream big. As a young girl growing up in a small town in Missouri, I had dreams of someday becoming a rock star. I love to sing and still do today. Using my jump rope for a microphone and singing to a crowd of toys, dolls, and teddy bears, at six-years-old, I was a rock star! And to this day, I can still hear that crowd roar.

As I grew older, I sang in a small band in high school. This allowed me to gain confidence in my abilities to sing. But there was much more to becoming a rock star than having confidence. I would also need the image, industry knowledge, hours of practice, and a strong desire.

Obviously, the career path that I had envisioned and desired in my youth changed as I grew older. Situations and life events led me in a different direction and ultimately changed my goals. But the importance of dreaming big has stuck with me throughout the years.

Maybe you are already a rock star in your career. Or maybe you have a different dream job in mind. We all have our own desires for our career. Finding your dream job can be a difficult, daunting task for some. Even the most qualified, ambitious candidates can have multiple interviews with several different organizations before they land their next position.

It's important to be patient. Patience is a virtue that many of us simply lack. We have needs, wants, and desires, and when things don't go as planned, we become frustrated. Frustration leads to further impatience, so the issue compounds itself. Organized people like to complete tasks. Finding a job has so many outside variables beyond our control, and dealing with that aspect is hard. You will garner success by systematically approaching your employment search, but it still takes time. Time is of the essence for many, and we're hoping you have collected some pearls along the way to help you land your dream job.

Yes, we've talked at great length in this book about what to do in your job search and how to prepare for interviews. But there are still other areas to consider in your quest to finding your dream job. Let's talk about a few of these and what you can do to stay positive during your job search.

First, don't become defeated. As stated earlier, it's not an easy task to find a great fit in your future employment. Days, weeks and sometimes months can go by in which you've worked very hard to land a position and still not received interview opportunities. It happens to the best of candidates. Keep your spirits up and remain positive. Opportunities do not always come at convenient times nor will they come on your schedule. Be flexible, motivated, yet relaxed in your job search. Your loved ones will appreciate it. We know that employment status doesn't simply impact a candidate; loved ones are affected too. If you need career advice from a professional, don't be afraid to reach out to one. Try to find a career counselor or coach who specializes in helping job seekers interested in your desired career path.

Secondly, don't lack enthusiasm. We mentioned this numerous times in the text, but it is truly a controllable element that should always be on your mind through every part of the interview process. Sometimes our feedback from clients include a commentary that the candidate was not engaged or highly motivated during the interview. You have control of that aspect of your persona.

Thirdly, don't limit the scope of your search or activities. Use all of your resources and, as the saying goes, keep many irons in the fire. Keep active in your searches and go out of your way to make yourself available for interviews. It will open you up to many more potential opportunities.

Finally, don't lack follow up. If you've interviewed or had an interaction with an influencer or decision maker, send them an appropriate thank-you note or follow-up email.

The acronym discussed in the book -- DESIRE -- is designed to help you gather your thoughts, design your strategies, and thereby greatly facilitate your job search. Ultimately, applying the elements of DESIRE should help you succeed in interviewing for current or future opportunities.

Recall that the word *desire* is colloquially defined as a strong feeling of wanting to have something or wishing for something to happen. Wishing is great, but you know you will have to work hard for your wish to come true. Few worthy dreams come true without a sincere effort.

If you approach your job search with confidence, clarity, conviction, and enthusiasm, you will see the impact that your attitude can make upon your employment outcome. Your strong motivation, in conjunction with the six-steps (DESIRE) described in this book can help take you across the finish line.

Over the years, we've talked to thousands of candidates that have helped us align these strategies to help candidates just like you. You are competing in the job market, and we want you to win.

We encourage you to use what you've learned here in our book, keep an open mind, and control what you can control. Sometimes it may seem that you are trekking up an insurmountable mountain, but if you pursue your employment search with diligence and motivation, your outcome can be a great reward.

Thanks for picking up our book. We hope we've helped you by providing a great insight into how to prepare and interview for your next job. Best of luck in your quest to find your dream job!

REFERENCES

(2020, April 22). Retrieved from Quotes:
    https://www.quotes.net/quote/2442

Davidson, P. (2018, July 19). *Workers are 'ghosting' interviews, blowing off work in a strong job market Assessed on 3/19/20.* Retrieved from USA Today: https://www.usatoday.com/story/money/2018/07/19/strong-job-market-candidates-ghosting-interviews-offers/794264002/

Disney Dreamer. (n.d.). *Walt Disney Quotes.* Retrieved from Disney Dreamer: https://www.disneydreamer.com/walt-disney-quotes-3/

Doyle, A. (2020, March 6). *How to Use the STAR Interview Response Method.* Retrieved from The Balance Careers: https://www.thebalancecareers.com/what-is-the-star-interview-response-technique-2061629

Forbes Quotes. (2020, 2 28). *Thoughts on the Business of Life.* Retrieved from https://www.forbes.com/quotes/10624/

Grensing-Pophal, L. (2020). If You Could Be Any Vegetable' and Other OffBeat Interview Questions. *HR Magazine*, 10.

Heslin, G. (2020, February 28). *Layoffs and Downsizing in 2007.* Retrieved from http://business-view-9-co.50webs.com/layoffs-and-downsizing-in-2007-261956.html

HR Dive. (2020, February 28). *Salary history bans: A running list of states and localities that have outlawed pay history questions. Accessed 3/19/20.* Retrieved from HR Dive: https://www.hrdive.com/news/salary-history-ban-states-list/516662/

Lewis, L. (2019, August 26). *The Ghosting Guide: An Inside Look at Why Job Seekers Disappear.* Retrieved from Indeed Blog: http://blog.indeed.com/2019/08/26/ghosting-guide/

Merriam Webster. (2019, July 8th). Retrieved from https://www.merriam-webster.com/dictionary/ghosting

Merriam-Webster Dictionary. (2020, May 9th). Retrieved from
    https://www.merriam-webster.com/dictionary/networking

Quote Investigator. (2020, March 16).
    https://quoteinvestigator.com/2010/05/17/remain-silent/

INDEX

Gut reaction · 3, 83

H

Hiring markets · 104
    candidate's market · 104
    employer's market · 104

I

Internship · 57
Interview process · 33, 90

J

Job offer · 2, 54, 79, 83, 91, 94
Job shadowing · 55

K

Kudos file folder · 73

L

LinkedIn · 21, 33, 43, 80, 111, 112, 113

N

Networking · 43, 108, 109, 110, 111, 113

W

Website, career · 80, 81

ABOUT THE AUTHORS

Denise Wilkerson is the founder and CEO of Global Edge Recruiting Associates, LLC. Randy Wilkerson, her husband and business partner, is the Vice-President of Executive Search and Recruitment Services. Founded in 1997, Global Edge Recruiting® is a nationally recognized executive search firm specializing in the recruitment of sales and marketing professionals for medical device, pharmaceutical, biotechnology, dental, and veterinary companies.

More About Denise Wilkerson

Born in NYC and raised in a small town in Missouri, Denise started her career in nursing – first in oncology, where she worked in the hospital as a staff nurse, and then for a hospice where she managed a team of nurses. After managing a large women's healthcare clinic for a local hospital, she decided to start her own business and opened Global Edge Recruiting in 1997. Since that time, Denise has assisted hundreds of Fortune 500 and small start-up companies by recruiting their top talent and assisting them with day-to-day human resource and organizational development needs.

Denise is also passionate about helping job seekers through various types of career transitions. As a career counselor, she assists job seekers with resume development, interviewing skills, and career management. Denise enjoys sharing her knowledge with others, which is evident by her company's blog and social media. She has contributed to multiple publications and books on recruitment.

On a professional note, Denise has a Bachelor's degree in Nursing, as well as a Master's in Human Resource Development and a Senior Professional Human Resources certification (SPHR). Her love for innovative medical products and devices, as well as her passion for assisting individuals with career development, led her to healthcare recruitment. She has over thirty years of hiring experience in general healthcare, sales and marketing.

More about Randy Wilkerson

A native of Springfield, Missouri, Randy is the son of two educators. His mother was a teacher and high school counselor in the Springfield area, and his father was a high school principal and state representative. As Randy was growing up, his parents emphasized the importance of education, something that has stuck with him throughout life.

While attending Missouri State University, Randy received a teaching certification in business and general science, along with his undergraduate degree in both marketing and management. Later, he completed his Masters of Business Administration at Webster University. He has a private pilot's license and a real estate broker's license. Randy loves to educate others along with being in front of a group. Early in his career, he taught adult education courses in real estate.

Randy Wilkerson joined Global Edge Recruiting in 2007 as Vice President, Executive Search and Recruitment. Prior to joining Global Edge, Randy was a successful sales representative. He worked for several Fortune 500 companies including Xerox Corporation, Roche Pharmaceuticals and Janssen Pharmaceuticals, a division of Johnson and Johnson. Randy's extensive background in sales and marketing assists clients in the recruitment and development of sales teams. Randy has over fifteen years of hiring experience in general healthcare sales and marketing.

Personally, Randy is known for his sense of humor, which is evident in many of his writings. He is also very technical and enjoys a good repair challenge. He rebuilds old jukeboxes and pinball machines for fun. In addition to these hobbies, he likes to spend time at the lake and working on the family's ranch.

For More Information, visit www.dandyworx.com

OTHER RESOURCES

**HIRE with FIRE: The Relationship-Driven
Interview and Hiring Method
Written by Denise and Randy Wilkerson**

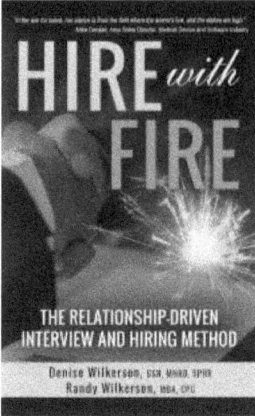

*Is there a correlation between finding your
perfect soul mate and finding the perfect
people to work for your company?*

*How does a candidate's interview experience
impact your employer brand?*

*Will their experience influence your ability to
attract top talent in the future?*

HIRE with FIRE provides a relationship-based hiring method to help you hire the best people and create an engaged workforce. Designed as an interview guide for hiring managers and human resource professionals, *HIRE with FIRE* will help your company improve the candidate experience, hire the best people, build your employer brand, attract top talent, retain top performers and create engaged employees.

WHO SHOULD READ *HIRE WITH FIRE*
Whether you are a CEO, an HR manager, experienced or new to hiring, HIRE with FIRE will show you how to hire the best people who will set your company apart from the competition.

Although geared toward the hiring authorities, those seeking employment can also gain a unique perspective into what employers want in their new employees.

Available in ebook, paperback, hardcover and audiobook.
ISBN-13: 978-1-7332611-04

ABOUT THE PUBLISHER

Dandyworx Productions, LLC publishes high-quality, non-fiction books designed to educate, inspire, and entertain the reader. Our editors are experienced professionals with years of leadership and hiring experience.

Dandyworx Productions is proud to offer books in the following categories:
> Business / Management / Leadership
> HR & Personnel Management
> Career Management

Through an expanded distribution network, our books are available at most retailers and independent bookstores. We offer a variety of formats, such as paperback, hardback, ebooks and audiobooks.

This book is available at quantity discounts for bulk purchases. For more information or permission to use copyrighted material, visit www.dandyworx.com

www.ingramcontent.com/pod-product-compliance
Lightning Source LLC
Chambersburg PA
CBHW021432180326
41458CB00001B/241